Gabriela Mistral

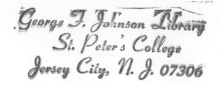
Gabriela Mistral

THE POET AND HER WORK

By *Margot Arce de Vazquez*

Translated by Helene Masslo Anderson

NEW YORK UNIVERSITY PRESS 1964

*The original Spanish edition of this book appeared
under the title* Gabriela Mistral Persona y Poesía
and was published by Ediciones Asomante, San Juan.

To her memory . . . .

CONTENTS

Gabriela Mistral

Biography

CHILDHOOD

Lucila Godoy Alcayaga, known to the world of letters as
"Gabriela Mistral," was born on April 7, 1889, in Vicuña, in the
small Elqui valley of northern Chile. Her father, Jerónimo Godoy
Vilanueva, married the widow Petronila Alcayaga de Molina,
who had a fifteen-year old daughter, Emelina, by her first marriage. Jerónimo Godoy was a strange man—vagabond, poet, and
former theological student—who was at that time an elementary
school teacher in the village of La Unión. Little Lucila's heritage
was a mixed one: Indian and perhaps Jewish on her father's
side, Basque on her mother's. From her father too she inherited
a talent for poetry, stirrings of religious feeling, and a wandering, anti-bourgeois spirit; from her mother, physical beauty and
an artistic temperament.

When she was barely three years old, her father deserted
their home and never returned. Her mother and half-sister, Emelina, dedicated themselves completely to the care and education
of the child. Since both were teachers, they gave her primary
instruction and, in addition, supported the household with what
they earned.

Up to 1901, Lucila's childhood was spent in the narrow An-
dean valley, in constant touch with the land and with nature's
beings all about her. She spent long hours in the orchard, talking
to the birds and the animals, gazing at the clouds, the stars, and
the constantly changing waters of the river. She was a timid,

quiet child given to dreaming. On Sundays, her paternal grandmother would read passages from the Bible and her mother and sister would tell her stories. She was extremely fond of imaginative literature and poetic and musical folklore; the readings from the Bible left a profound impression on her spirit and on her poetry.

Emelina was her first teacher. She took Lucila to school with her and taught her reading, writing, and her very first concepts of geography and history. At school Lucila's timidity and withdrawn character created difficulties for her. Her teachers thought her dull; some of them advised her mother to train her for domestic duties. Her classmates took advantage of her, but she never complained nor did she ever say a word in her own defense. Once in Vicuña, Lucila acted as aide and secretary to a blind teacher who put her in charge of distributing class materials; since she tended to be absent-minded, the students stole all they could from her. When the teacher discovered the theft, she accused Lucila and expelled her from school. Her classmates, waiting outside, threw stones at her as she passed. This cruel experience marked the end of her childhood. It was an experience that left a lingering, painful imprint on her memory and sensitivity.

PROFESSIONAL LIFE

In spite of everything, Lucila's mother and sister continued to prepare her for teaching. They had faith in her and considered no effort or sacrifice too great to insure the continuation of the necessary studies. Moving to La Serena, they applied for her admission to the normal school there. At about this time, Lucila began to write for the local newspapers. She published poems and prose articles in which she freely expounded her Socialist philosophy and her admiration for Vargas Vila, the controversial Colombian writer. The chaplain of the normal school rejected her application, claiming that her ideas could harm the students. Emelina and her mother were not deterred by this setback and through their tutoring helped her finish her course of study. Since 1904 she had been working as a teacher's assistant in a rural school at La Cantera. With the award of her official certificate of study in 1910, she was finally able to hold positions in high schools throughout the country: La Serena, Traiguén, los Andes, Antofogasta, Temuco, Punta Arenas, and Santiago, the highest rung on the ladder—always with the encouragement and moral support of her friends, Fidela Pérez Valdés and Pedro Aguirre La Cerda, who was later to become president of Chile. By 1912 she was well settled in Santiago, her pedagogical work recognized not only in her own country but even beyond its borders. She lived on the outskirts of the capital, visited at all hours by writers, artists, workers, ladies of Santiago's aristocracy, and students. Her time was devoted to studies and readings in theosophy and to the practice of yoga; she carried on a correspondence with Annie Besant and Amado Nervo, the Mexican poet, who was also interested in these pursuits.

For her, teaching was a calling to which she gave all her enthusiasm, freedom, and a creative spirit that abhorred routine. A large proportion of her literary work, both prose and poetry, had an educational purpose; it was intended for the classroom and was written with a view to awakening and forming within the child a moral and religious conscience and an aesthetic sensitivity. In the classroom she was a severe taskmaster, exacting hard work and strict discipline.

The culmination of her teaching career was in June 1922, when José Vasconcelos, Mexico's Secretary of Education, officially invited her to collaborate with him in a program of educational reform that he was about to undertake in his country. Gabriela accepted and left for the Mexican capital, where she resided until 1924. There she became especially interested in the teaching of Indians in rural areas; she wanted to "infuse teaching with an apostolic and spiritual feeling." The experience in Mexico was a decisive one in her moral and intellectual life. She visited every corner of that beautiful country and came to know and admire the Mexican Indian. She regained her Catholic faith, established lasting friendships with Palma Guillén, Alfonso Reyes, Antonio Castro Leal, Pedro Henríquez Ureña, Enrique González Martínez, and, in addition, published her anthology, *Readings for Women* (*Lecturas para mujeres*). The love and memory of Mexico and of her Mexican friends stayed with her until her death.

In 1923, Chile awarded her the title of "Teacher of the Nation." On March 4, 1925, after twenty-one years of outstanding service, she accepted retirement.

EMOTIONAL LIFE

At the very beginning of her academic work, while a teacher in La Cantera in 1907, she experienced first love. His name was Romelio Ureta, an employee of the railroad company. Their relationship was marred by frequent and bitter disputes due to sharp differences of opinion. They finally severed their relationship and parted. In 1909, Ureta committed suicide for reasons of personal honor having nothing to do with his former betrothal. A search of his body revealed a postal card from Gabriela in the jacket pocket. The circumstances of Ureta's death left an indelible impression on the young school teacher. Many of her poems written in those years speak of love, sorrow, and death.

On December 22, 1914, she competed in the poetic Floral Games in Santiago with her "Sonnets of Death" (*Sonetos de la Muerte*), dedicated to the memory of Ureta's tragic death. With them she won the Gold Medal. Gabriela attended the presentation of awards incognito, hidden among the people who had filled the room. She was at that time a young girl of twenty-five, tall, slim, with a pale complexion, smooth golden hair, and green eyes, bright yet with a longing in them. Her proud bearing, her somewhat abstracted, distant air gave her an aura of loneliness and mystery. One of her colleagues, quoting a line from the Chilean national anthem, described her as "majestic, the white mountain" (*majestuosa la blanca montaña*). All of this enhanced both her fame as a poet and the magnetic attraction that her personality exercised on all who knew her.

Shortly after this first literary triumph, she met under romantic and somewhat strange circumstances a young poet from Santiago; for him she felt a passion much deeper, more intense and more decisive than her first love. A short while later, however, he married a wealthy young lady of the capital's high social circles. The cruel blow moved her to ask for her transfer to Punta Arenas in the extreme south of Chile, an inhospitable, desolate region. There she remained for two years, exiled and overwhelmed with sorrow. It was then, having decided to leave Chile, that she accepted the invitation from the Mexican government. The most moving and impassioned poems of *Desolation* (*Desolación*), the very title of that anguished book, express with ardent eloquence her heartbreaking disillusion. She turned her gaze to children and wrote for them, transforming her frustrated longing for motherhood into tenderness. In her affection for the American lands and peoples and in the pleasures of friendship she sought the companionship denied to her by love. She adopted her nephew, Juan Miguel Godoy, and raised him as a son. But in friendship she was also to know cruel blows; while in Brazil, she was shattered by the suicide of her dear friends, Stefan Zweig and his young wife, as well as that of Juan Miguel, on August 13, 1943. From the date of that event her physical health began to fail. Plunged into sorrow, she waited for death.

LITERARY LIFE

Gabriela's literary calling became evident very early in life. At 16 she was already writing for the newspapers and journals of her native region. Gradually she became known for her anti-bourgeois social ideas and for her verses influenced by Modernism. Professor Manuel Gómez Maturana's inclusion of some of her prose and poetry in his *Books for Reading* (*Libros de Lectura*) brought her to the attention of the intellectual circles of Chile. She also began to win fame abroad, both for the writings she published in the press and for the correspondence she carried on with notable Hispanic-American writers, among them Rubén Darío himself. The prize she won in 1914 at the Floral Games of Santiago and the trip to Mexico consolidated her national and inter-American reputation.

In February 1921, Federico de Onís, a professor at Columbia University and an excellent critic, lectured on Gabriela Mistral's poetic work to a group of North American professors. On their initiative, her poems were compiled and published. Thus in 1922, the Hispanic Institute of New York published the first edition of Desolation (*Desolación*). With this publication the literary name of Gabriela Mistral definitively replaced her own name of Lucila Godoy Alcayaga.

The adoption of this pseudonymn revealed, as always occurs in these cases, something of her conception of the world and of man: "Gabriela," for the archangel Gabriel, divine messenger of good news; "Mistral," for the strong hot wind of Provence. Both components contained spiritual symbols. It was Gabriela's custom to classify people into three groups: children of air, of water, and of fire. Those of *air* were the intelligent ones, distinguished by their grace and spirit; she believed firmly in the archangels as creatures of pure spirit and intelligence and as mediators between God and men.

After Desolation (*Desolación*) there were long intervals between the publication of her other books of verses: Tenderness (*Ternura*), 1924; Felling (*Tala*), 1938. She was, however, constantly publishing new poems in the Hispanic-American press, and she began extensive and continuous journalistic work as a correspondent for the principal journals and newspapers of the Americas: *El Mercurio* of Chile, *La Nación* and *Crítica* of Argentina, *El Tiempo* of Colombia, *El Universal* of Caracas, *El Universal* of Mexico, *Sur* of Buenos Aires, *Atenea* of Chile, *Repertorio Americano* of Costa Rica, *Revista Bimestre Cubana* of Cuba, *Puerto Rico Illustrado*, and *La nueva democracia*.

Her journalistic work was initiated in the local press of Chile in about 1907 and, after extending through all Hispano-America, it continued without interruption for about fifty years until her her death in 1957. Most of these contributions were written in prose that had a personal accent and style, as beautiful and interesting as her poetry. When she was in foreign countries—Spain, France, Italy, Portugal, Brazil, the United States—she also contributed to the newspapers and her articles were translated into the respective national languages.

Her articles for the press dealt with the most varied themes: contemporary events, persons, places and things, literary criticism, social, political, moral, religious, pedagogical, and aesthetic questions. Her pen was always at the service of truth, goodness, justice, liberty, and peace and was inspired by a Christian and democratic humanism.

Perhaps it was the profound value of her poetry as a work of art and as a human document and of her prose as an expression of values essential to contemporary man that won for her the highest literary award in the world, the Nobel Prize for Literature, presented to her in Sweden on November 15, 1945. She was both the first woman and the first Hispanic-American writer to receive this high universal recognition.

During the last twelve years of her life she continued to write poetry and prose for the newspapers in spite of her pitiful spiritual state and the illness that sapped her physical energies. In 1951, while in Rapallo, she received the National Award for Chilean Literature. In 1954 she published her last book, *Wine Press* (*Lagar*), and was preparing a "Song to Chile" (*Canto a Chile*), a long poem of eulogy and love for her country, which remains partially unpublished.

DIPLOMATIC POSTS; TRAVELS

The period of Gabriela's travels through Europe and America, of her service in the Chilean Consular Corps, and of her collaboration in cooperative intellectual world organizations dates from her departure from Chile for Mexico in 1922.

In 1924 she left Mexico for the United States where, at the Washington, D. C., Pan American Union, she delivered a speech on the brotherhood of the Americas. This was followed by a visit to several European countries: Italy, Switzerland, France, Spain. In 1926, as a member of the Committee for Intellectual Cooperation of the League of Nations, with headquarters in Paris, she took charge of the section of Hispanic-American literature. She published a collection of Hispanic-American classics translated into French in careful critical editions, with prologues, annotations and, in some cases, with glossaries. She was also a member of the Educational Cinematographic Institute of Rome. For a while she lived in Bedarrides, a little town in Provence. Between 1930 and 1931 she visited the United States, Puerto Rico, Cuba, Santo Domingo, Panamá, Guatemala, and El Salvador.

Although the Chilean government appointed her honorary consul in Naples, she was refused the *Exequatur* by Mussolini because of some anti-Fascist articles she had written. She returned to Puerto Rico in 1933 and taught a course in Hispanic-American literature at the University of Puerto Rico. There she was awarded the degree of *Doctor Honoris Causa* and delivered the address at the conferral of degrees. The Puerto Rican legislature bestowed upon her the title "adopted daughter of Puerto Rico."

Between 1934 and 1935 she was in Madrid as honorary consul, going from there to Lisbon as Consul *Vitalicio*, second class, with the right to choose her place of residence. In 1937 she visited France, Germany, and Denmark; in August she returned to South America and visited Brazil, Uruguay, Argentina, Chile, Perú, Ecuador, Panamá, and Cuba. Everywhere both intellectuals and the people received her with great enthusiasm when she gave lectures in the educational and literary centers. After spending six months in Cuba, she went to Florida and then to Washington.

In December 1938, she was appointed Chilean Consul in Nice, but the European crisis that unleashed World War II made her decide to request transfer to Brazil.

She lived in Brazil from 1939 to 1945, first in Niteroi and later in Petrópolis. Overwhelmed by the suicide of her nephew, Juan Miguel, she left for Europe at the end of 1945. In Stockholm she received the Nobel Prize, and following the reception she visited England, France, and Italy. She was awarded an honorary doctoral degree by the University of Florence and was received in private audience by Pope Pius XII.

She returned to the United States as Chilean Consul in Los Angeles. While in California, she lived first in Monrovia and then in Santa Barbara, in a lovely house with a garden and orchard. Columbia University and the University of California awarded her honorary degrees. Stricken with diabetes she went to Mexico to convalesce at the invitation of President Aleman and was presented with a house and land in Veracruz by the Mexican government. In 1951 she returned to Naples where she received the National Award for Chilean Literature. In 1953 she went to Cuba to take part in the ceremonies of

Martí's centennial celebration. From there she moved to New York as Chilean delegate to the United Nations and participated in the colloquia on the freedom of culture at Columbia University.

The state of her health forced her to resign from her post at the United Nations and to retire to Roslyn Bay, Long Island, where she had lived since 1954 in the company of her friend, Doris Dana.

On January 10, 1957, she died of cancer of the pancreas in Hempstead Hospital, Long Island. The funeral services were held in St. Patrick's Cathedral in New York and her remains moved to Chile, to Montegrande in the Elqui valley, where they now rest.

Life and Poetry

ONE of the most delicate and fascinating problems for the student of literature is the relationship that exists between the life of a poet and his work; how to determine which element of his poetry is pure creation and which simple biography. The question becomes even more complicated when, in addition to knowing the body of work objectively, one has also had intimate, daily contact with the poet. For then, at each moment, one runs the risk of looking for hidden meanings, of overestimating the significance of gestures, acts, and words and of coming to believe that, without great effort, one has hit upon the key to the poetic mystery. There finally comes the moment when history and poetry seem to merge in such a way that one feels totally incapable of separating them and assessing the true value of each.

Such was our experience with Gabriela Mistral. We lived closely together for varying periods of time and, on one occasion, for an entire year. Her case was more difficult because most of the time she seemed to spend her days in a world of poetic illusion, although sometimes she would return to reality suddenly and move within it with the most disconcerting aplomb. Those who had seen her lose herself in stone-like impassivity for long periods of time were unable to reconcile this with her ease in the treatment of things and her vivacious manner with people.

Gabriela was scarcely one of those poets who do not seem to be a part of their verse, who give the impression of donning their poetry when they feel the impulse and removing it, as one removes an article of clothing that does not quite fit. The Gabriela revealed to us in her work, the image of her that the reader gradually forms, could be twin to the real Gabriela. Only the most careful observer would detect the slight differences. But the traits they share are there as a kind of consoling evidence; consoling because Gabriela Mistral, the great poet, was at the same time one of the most noble and just individuals that it has been our good fortune to know. Her integrity as a human being alone would suffice to place her far above others. It is not a small matter that poetry can endure in this fashion: in the words of Cervantes, to shine with the brilliance of a magic helmet without suddenly having it revert to a barber's basin. When, at the end of the war, Gabriela was awarded the Nobel Prize for Literature, it occurred to us that perhaps the Swedish Academy, in this century of terrible and decisive trial for intellectuals, wanted to honor this fidelity of life and work in which poetry and truth, hand in hand, take nourishment from the same sources.

We first met Gabriela Mistral in Madrid, in the autumn of 1928. We still remember clearly that brief encounter in the golden garden of the young women's International House. Some of us had been talking together under the trees when she came toward us with her remote air and her tiredness of centuries. The woolen cape that fell to below her knees accentuated her undulating movement like that of the eddying of a river; the radiance of her sharply etched head compensated for the stolidity of her body. Her eyes and mouth seemed to contradict each other: a mouth bitter with worldly knowledge, the eyes serene and inquisitive. We could not help but contrast this figure with the one we had imagined from the verses of *Desolation (Desolación)*; there was something disturbing about that idol-like immobility, that way she had of removing herself from everything, of withdrawing within herself as if she were listening to an inner voice, unique among all other voices. The lines of Antonio Machado suddenly came to mind:

> I speak with the man who always walks my way,
> He who speaks alone hopes to speak with God one day.

Afterwards we could see that God was the constant thought, the daily preoccupation of Gabriela Mistral; God, love, and America.

There was one other Spanish-American resident besides myself at the International House then. At suppertime Gabriela requested that we be seated next to her. Her conversation revealed to us her total love for America—her nostalgia for the lands, the countrysides, and the people. We spoke of nothing else. Several years of absence from the Americas had produced an almost physical longing within her; she was haunted by insistent, pervasive images. She spoke of Mexico, Cuba, and Chile; she asked about Puerto Rico. She felt strange in that Spanish atmosphere and geography. She longed for her Chilean valleys, the mountain range, the tropical sun. Like Anteu, she needed to draw strength from the peaks of her Elqui valley, or the Mexican cornfields. In a stanza of her "Hymn to the Sun," she has expressed this debilitation of her entire being when in exile:

Pisé los cuarzos extranjeros,	I trod on foreign soils,
comí sus frutos mercenarios;	Their mercenary fruits did
en mesa dura y vaso sordo	eat;
bebí hidromieles que eran	On hard table and in dull
lánguidos;	glass
recé oraciones mortecinas	I drank their weakened mead;
y me canté los himnos	I murmured dying prayers
bárbaros,	And to myself barbaric hymns
y dormí donde son dragones	I sang
rotos y muertos los Zodíacos.	And slept where the Zodiacs
	Are dead and dragons broken.

In "The Stranger" (*La Extranjera*), a magnificent moral self-portrait, she insists on speaking of her "apartness," the constant sensation of strangeness and isolation with which she lived for several years in a small Provencal village:

—Habla con dejo de sus mares bárbaros
con no sé qué algas y no sé qué arenas;
reza oración a Dios sin bulto y peso,
envejecida como si muriera.
En huerto nuestro que nos hizo extraño,
ha puesto cactus y zarpadas hierbas.
Alienta del resuello del desierto
y ha amado con pasión de que blanquea,
que nunca cuenta y que si nos contase

sería como el mapa de otra estrella.
Vivirá entre nosotros ochenta años,
pero siempre será como si llega,
hablando lengua que jadea y gime
y que le entienden sólo bestezuelas.
Y va a morirse en medio de nosotros,
en una noche en la que más padezca,
con sólo su destino por almohada,
de una muerte callada y extranjera.

She speaks in her way of her savage seas
With unknown algae and unknown sands;
She prays to a formless, weightless God,
Aged, as if dying.
In our garden now so strange,
She has planted cactus and alien grass.
The desert zephyr fills her with its breath
And she has loved with a fierce, white passion
She never speaks of, for if she were to tell
It would be like the face of unknown stars.
Among us she may live for eighty years,
Yet always as if newly come,
Speaking a tongue that pants and whines
Only by tiny creatures understood.
And she will die here in our midst
One night of utmost suffering,
With only her fate as a pillow,
And death, silent and strange.

These lines might well have been spoken by her, for her feeling
for America had in actuality the same poetic quality it has in
her books. The elements of fiction and metaphor we note here
were also present when she spoke in prose and without any
deliberate artistic aim.

Almost all of the American poems in *Felling (Tala)* date
from her years of residence in Europe. Her home then was a
refuge and mecca for all Spanish-Americans who happened to
be passing through, no matter what their native lands. For
Gabriela, national differences did not exist where America was
concerned; her wish was for one great unit extending from
Mexico to Patagonia, with one common citizenship. True to this
concept, her Chilean consulate served the Venezuelan as well
as the Paraguayan or the Guatemalan. The Puerto Ricans who
were studying in Madrid when she was consul knew her hos-

pitality and her active interest in them and in Puerto Rico. She never refused them help, whether in small or large matters.

Gabriela's broad sense of America superseded any excessive, foolishly sentimental love of country. During the territorial dispute between Peru and Chile, she had the moral courage to condemn publicly Chile's conduct and support the stand of the Peruvians, who were in the right. The anger of her countrymen did not matter to her; what mattered above all was justice. Out of that same sense of justice has come a song to the liberty of Puerto Rico, in a poem filled with tenderness:

Mar Caribe	Caribbean Sea
Isla en caña y cafés	Island in cane and coffees
apasionada;	passionate,
tan dulce de decir	So sweet to speak of
como una infancia;	like a childhood,
¡bendita de cantar	Blessed with song
como un hosanna!	like a hosanna!
Sirena sin canción	Siren without song
sobre las aguas	upon the waters,
ofendida de mar	Offended by the sea
en marejada:	in swell of surf:
¡Cordelia de las olas	Cordelia of the waves,
Cordelia amarga!	bitter Cordelia!
Seas salvada como	May you be saved
la corza blanca	like the white roe deer
y como el llama neuvo	like the new llama
del Pachacámac,	of Pachacámac,
y como el huevo de oro	and like the golden egg
de la nidada,	of the brood,
y como la Ifigenia,	And like Iphigenia,
viva en la llama.	alive in the flame.

Significantly, the poem is dated Independence Day of the Philippines. In contrast to the ruggedness of the Andes and the powerful landscape of the Continent, it was the softness and sweetness of the Puerto Rican atmosphere that attracted her:

Beber	Drink
En la isla de Puerto Rico	On the island of Puerto Rico
a la siesta de azul colmada	Brimming with blue at siesta
mi cuerpo quieto, las olas locas,	time,
y como cien madres las palmas,	My body still, the waves wild,

rompió una niña por donaire
junto a mi boca un coco de agua
y yo bebí como una hija
agua de madre, agua de palma.
¡Y más dulzura no he bebido
con el cuerpo ni con el alma!

And like a hundred mothers the
    palms,
A child gracefully opened beside
    my lips,
A coconut filled with milk,
And I drank as a daughter takes
Mother's milk, the milk of
    palms.
And never have I drunk more
    sweetness
Neither with body or with soul.

Her love for Mexico had other roots: the beauty of the country, the uniqueness of its indigenous culture, the loyal friendships of Palma Guillén, Alfonso Reyes, and Daniel Cossío Villegas; the sense of identity with blood and race:

Beber	Drink
En el campo de Mitla un día	On the field of Mitla one day
de cigarras, de sol, de marcha	Of cicadas, sun and movement
me doblé a un pozo y vino un	I bent over a well and an Indian
indio	came
a sostenerme sobre el agua	To hold me over the water
y mi cabeza, como un fruto,	And my head like a fruit,
estaba dentro de sus palmas.	Lay within his palms.
Bebía yo lo que bebía	I drank what he drank
que era su cara con mi cara,	And his face and mine were one,
y en un relámpago yo supe	And in a flash I knew
carne de Mitla ser mi casta.	That flesh of Mitla was my flesh.

If in her American fervor Gabriela went beyond national borders to embrace the entire continent, in her charity and love of culture, all frontiers everywhere were erased. We remember, for example, how she rose to the defense of the Italians, when, after Guadalajara, all Italians were jeered at without distinction, without anyone attempting to explain their supposed cowardice.

One could say a great deal about Gabriela's contradictory feelings toward Spain. The evils of the conquest and colonization of America and the mistreatment of the Indians by the Spanish settlers angered her to the point of losing all equanimity. Several times she argued this empassioned question with her friends. We used to tell her that her antagonism was born of a great similarity of temperament and that no mater how much Indian blood she had, hers was predominantly a Spanish heritage. She

would become extremely irritated and would never admit it.
Once we presented her with some records of Castilian folksongs
and wrote down for her the words to some popular songs. As she
heard again those rhythms, that poetry, that gift for grace, the
classical, poetic expression, she began to make her definitive
peace with the Spanish. Later, in 1937, when she met José
Bergamín, Joaquín Xirau, Victoria Kent, and Carlos Rivas in
Paris, she was completely won over. She finally told us: "Look,
my daughter, when these people are fine there is no doubt that
they are the aristocrats of the world." And then, with the same
passion she gave to everything, she devoted herself to helping
the Spanish people in their fight against Fascism. She would stay
awake for nights on end thinking of the children, suffering for
those who were dying on the battlefields or under German
bombs. Within a short time her room at the hotel Montpensier
became the gathering place for the Spaniards who were in Paris
during those tragic days when there was still some hope. Out
of her nightly vigils and concern came the gift of *Felling* (*Tala*)
to the children's camp of Pedralbes.

There is always some event which draws out of me the book that
I would have left for the calends because of creole neglect. The
first time it was Professor Onís and the Spanish professors of the
United States who overcame my laxness and published *Desolation*
(*Desolación*); now, I offer *Felling* (*Tala*), because I have nothing
else to give the Spanish children scattered to the four winds of the
world.
    Let them take the poor book from the hands of their Gabriela,
a *mestiza* [half-breed] born of Basques, and let the essential misery
in *Tala* be cleansed by this gesture of service born of my love for
the innocent blood of Spain that is wandering now across the
Peninsula and through the whole of Europe.
    It is a source of overwhelming amazement to me, I would even
say of acute shame, to see my Spanish America with her arms
folded, in the face of the tragedy of the Basque children. In the
physical breadth and the generosity of nature found on our Continent, there was more than enough room to have taken them all
in, sparing them sojourns in countries of impossible language, of
bitter climates and among strange peoples. This time the ocean
has not been an instrument of our charity, and our beaches, which
have welcomed the most dubious immigrations, have not provided
a landing place for the feet of the wandering children of the un-
fortunate Basque country. We the Basques and half-Basques of

America have accepted the dispersal of these children of our blood and in each morning's paper we have read, without our hearts stirring, the heartrending tales of the haggling of some countries over the admission of the shiploads of fugitives or orphans. For the first time in my life, I do not understand my people; their moral attitude truly stupifies me.

Months later, in Lisbon, we saw her risk her personal safety to defend a Spanish Republican who was a complete stranger to her. When we became a bit frightened at her imprudent actions, she reproached us for what she called our "indolence of spirit." "See the Christian ladies doubting while the life of a man is in danger!" And her splendid charity and passion for justice spread to everyone.

This was the kind of woman she was: attentive to the present, dominated by the conscience of her deeds and of the course that history takes, incapable of refusing the claims of those who suffer from hunger or thirst for justice and love. If we read her work carefully, we will find embodied there the same concepts and attitudes, and it would almost be impossible to distinguish between art and life or to say if there is more authentic poetry in her verses than in her acts. Everything she did, said, and wrote was in some way saturated with that poetic air, revealing the marvelous, if somewhat delicate, balance between the "is" and the "should be." Several poems in *Felling* (*Tala*) embody this harmony, in which the ethical, the aesthetic, and the religious are fused with subtlety. "Bread" (*Pan*), for example:

> *Dejaron un pan en la mesa,*
> *mitad quemado, mitad blanco,*
> *pellizcado encima y abierto*
> *en unos migajones de ampo.*
>
> *Me parece nuevo o como no visto*
> *y otra cosa que él no me ha alimentado*
> *pero volteando su miga, sonámbula,*
> *tacto y olor se me olvidaron.*
>
> *Huele a mi madre cuando dió su leche,*
> *huele a tres valles por donde he pasado:*
> *a Aconcagua, a Pázcuaro, a Elqui,*
> *y a mis entrañas cuando yo canto.*
>
> *Otros olores no hay en la estancia*
> *y por eso él así me ha llamado;*

y no hay nadie tampoco en la casa
sino este pan abierto en un plato,
que con su cuerpo me reconoce
y con el mío yo reconozco.

Se ha comido en todos los climas
el mismo pan en cien hermanos:
pan de Coquimbo, pan de Oaxaca,
pan de Santa Ana y de Santiago.

En mis infancias yo le sabía
forma de sol, de pez o de halo,
y sabía mi mano su miga
y el calor de pichón emplumado.

Después lo olvidé, hasta este día
en que los dos nos encontramos,
yo con mi cuerpo de Sara vieja
y él con el suyo de cinco años.

Amigos muertos con que comíalo
en otros valles, sientan el vaho
de un pan en septiembre molido
y en agosto en Castilla segado.

Es otro y es el que comimos
en tierras donde se acostaron.
Abro la miga y les doy su calor;
lo volteo y les pongo su hálito.

La mano tengo de él rebosada
y la mirada puesta en mi mano;
entrego un llanto arrepentido
por el olvido de tantos años,
y la cara se me envejece
o me renace en este hallazgo.

Como se halla vacía la casa,
estemos juntos los reencontrados,
sobre esta mesa sin carne y fruta,
los dos en este silencio humano
hasta que seamos otra vez uno
y nuestro día haya acabado . . .

On the table they left a bread,
Half of it burnt, half white,
Pinched on the top and opened
To its soft and snowy whiteness.

It seems new to me as if never before seen
And as if it has never nourished me
But turning its softness, dreamily
Touch and smell are forgotten.

It smells of my mother when she gave her milk,
It smells of three valleys through which I have passed:
Aconcagua, Pázcuaro, Elqui,
And of my womb when I sing.

In the room there is no other fragrance
That is why it has called to me so;
Nor is there anyone in the house
Save this opened bread upon a plate,
That with its body seems to know me
And I with mine.

This same bread in hundred kind
Has been eaten in all climes:
Bread of Coquimbo, bread of Oaxaca,
Bread of Santa Ana and of Santiago.
In my childhood days I knew its
Form of sun, of fish or halo,
And my hand knew its softness
And its warmth of feathered pigeon.

Afterwards I forgot it, until this day
In which again we both did meet,
I with my body of aged Sarah
And he with his of five years old.

Dead friends with whom I ate it
In other valleys, sense the aroma
Of a bread ground in September
and in August reaped in Castile.

It is another and yet the same we ate
In lands in which they went to sleep.
I open the bread and give them its warmth;
I turn it and lay before them its scent.

My hand is overflowing with it
and my look fixed on my hand;
I abandon myself to repentant tears
For the forgetfulness of so many years,
And my face is grown old
Or reborn in this encounter.

In this empty house
Let us stay together, reunited

On this table without meat or fruit,
We two in this human silence
Until we once again are one
And our day has ended.

We saw her live this same rapture at every moment. The only difference was in the rhythm of the words; but the quality and the hue of the experience were identical. There was an anecdote she used to relate to laugh a bit at her own absent-mindedness, but which seems to be significant proof of all we have just said.

In the patio of the school for girls in Santiago there grew an orange tree laden with friut. Looking at it one day Gabriela gave orders that not a single orange was to be touched. She wished to come every afternoon to delight in its beauty. The next morning the secretary of the school cut off the oranges and with them prepared the dessert that was to be eaten at lunch. Late in the afternoon Gabriela returned to the garden and sat down facing the tree with the same rapture as on the preceding day. "What are you doing, Miss Lucila?" "Here, looking at my oranges." "But Miss Lucila, what oranges? I cut them all off and you ate them in your dessert today." The real tree had disappeared: in its place Gabriela kept seeing only the beautiful image of the orange tree with its golden, rounded fruit.

Gabriela was to Spanish-America what Unamuno was to modern Spain. She represented the basic and typical essence of our race as Unamuno represented that which was typically Spanish. She carried within her a fusion of Basque and Indian heritage: Spanish in her rebellious, individualistic spirit; very Indian in her long, deep silences and in that priestly aura of stone idol. To this representative cultural value must be added the great value of her literary work, an incomparable document for what it reveals of her person and for its unique American accent.

Poetry

GABRIELA MISTRAL's poetry stands as a reaction to the Modernism of the Nicaraguan poet Rubén Darió (*rubendarismo*): a poetry without ornate form, without linguistic virtuosity, without evocations of gallant or aristocratic eras; it is the poetry of a rustic soul, as primitive and strong as the earth, of pure accents without the elegantly correct echoes of France. By comparison with Hispanic-American literature generally, which on so many occasions has been an imitator of European models, Gabriela's poetry possesses the merit of consummate originality, of a voice of its own, authentic and consciously realized. The affirmation within this poetry of the intimate "I," removed from everything foreign to it, makes it profoundly human, and it is this human quality that gives it its universal value.

Passion is its great central poetic Theme; sorrowful passion similar in certain aspects—in its obsession with death, in its longing for eternity—to Unamuno's agony; the result of a tragic love experience. *Pathos* has saturated the ardent soul of the poet to such an extent that even her concepts, her reasons are transformed into vehement passion. The poet herself defines her lyric poetry as "a wound of love inflicted on us by things." It is an instinctive lyricism of flesh and blood, in which the subjective, bleeding experience is more important than form, rhythm, or ideas. It is a truly pure poetry because it goes directly to the innermost regions of the spirit and springs from a fiery and violent heart.

The second important poetic motif is *nature*, or rather, *crea-*

21

tion, because Gabriela sings to every creation: to man, animals, vegetables, and minerals; to active and inert materials; and to objects made by human hands. All beings have for her a concrete, palpable reality and, at the same time, a magic existence that surrounds them with a luminous aura. In a single moment she reveals the unity of the cosmos, her personal relationship with creatures, and that state of mystic, Franciscan rapture with which she gathers them all to her.

There is also an abundance of poems fashioned after children's folklore. The stories, rounds, and lullabies, the poems intended for the spiritual and moral formation of the students, achieve the intense simplicity of true songs of the people; there throbs within them the sharp longing for motherhood, the inverted tenderness of a very feminine soul whose innermost "reason for being" is unfulfilled. These children's poems are found in all her books as a repeated poetic motif. Gabriela deftly approaches the soul of the child avoiding the great danger of the adult point of view. The marvellous narrative, the joy of free imagination, the affectionate, rhythmic language that at various times seems outcry, hallelujah, or riddle, all make of these poems authentic children's poetry, the most beautiful that has emerged from the lips of any American or Spanish poet.

Gabriela also expresses her love for school and for her work as a teacher. In the verses dealing with these themes, we can perceive her conception of pedagogy. She viewed teaching as a Christian duty and exercise of charity; its function was to awaken within the soul of the student religious and moral conscience and the love of beauty; it was a task carried out always under the gaze of God. More than twenty years of teaching deepened her capacity for understanding and her social, human concern. She never permitted her spirit to harden in a fatiguing and desensitizing routine. When there is a glimmer of pedagogy in her verses, it appears redeemed by fervor.

Her love and praise of American lands, memories of her Elqui valley, of Mexico's Indians, and of the sweet landscape of tropical islands, and her concern for the historical fate of these peoples form another insistent leit-motif of her poetry. No other poet, with the exception of Neruda in his songs to the Chilean land, has spoken with more emotion of the beauty of the American world and of the splendor of its nature.

Gabriela also wrote prose—pure creole prose, clothed in the sensuality of these lands, in their strength and sweetness; baroque Spanish, but a baroque more of tension and accent than language. She used this pithy, exaggerated, persuasive, frequently sharp prose for the work—her great ideal—of the solidarity of Hispanic nations. Once again one notes her kinship with Unamuno because Gabriela wished for a Hispanic-American union based on the common language, on a re-evaluation of the past that would fuse the Indian and Spanish heritage, and, above all, on moral strength and the critical examination of the present. Although she did not take part in politics, because as a woman she detested exhibitionistic feminism, her voice was heeded because of its great moral prestige. She never sold her pen to dictators, she never floundered. Her fearless and unhesitating defense of justice, liberty, and peace was especially admirable at a time when the defense of those values, thanks to the evil cunning of dangerous, modern nominalism, was looked upon with suspicion and fear.

Gabriela has left us an abundant body of poetic work gathered together in several books or scattered in newspapers and magazines throughout Europe and America. There surely exist numerous manuscripts of unpublished poems that should be compiled, catalogued, and published in a posthumous book. Gabriela wrote constantly, she corrected a great deal, and she was a bit lax in publishing. Like Góngora, she did not take much care in the preservation and filing of her papers. Once in a while we put them in order for her; we were certain that within a short time they would revert to their initial chaotic state. Sixteen years elapsed between *Desolation* (*Desolación*) and *Felling* (*Tala*); another sixteen, between *Felling* and *Wine Press* (*Lagar*). Each one of these books is the result of a selection that omits much of what was written during those long lapses of time. The time has now come to consider the compilation of her complete works; but to gather together so much material will be a slow, arduous task that will require the careful, critical polishing of texts.

For the study of her poetic work, there are presently available five published books that trace the evolution of her poetry.

1. *Desolación* (Desolation), New York: Hispanic Institute, 1922.

2. *Ternura* (Tenderness), 4th edition, corrected and enlarged. Buenos Aires: Espasa-Calpe, 1945, Vol. 503 of the Colección Austral. (The first edition is from Madrid, Saturnino Calleja, 1924.)

3. *Tala* (Felling), Buenos Aires: Sur, 1938.

4. *Anthology*, Santiago, Chile: Zig-Zag, 1941.

5. *Lagar* (Wine Press), Santiago, Chile: Ediciones del Pacífico, 1954.

The little volume dedicated to Gabriela in the collection, *The Best Lyric Poetry by the Best Poets* (*Las mejores poesías* (*líricas*) *de los mejores poetas*), published in Barcelona by Cervantes, reproduces poems from *Desolation* (*Desolación*). *White Clouds* (*Nubes Blancas*), published in Barcelona by B. Bauzá (Apollo Collection) is a clandestine edition of selections from *Desolation* and *Tenderness* (*Ternura*). Both publications shed little light on her work; they add nothing new to what has already been published. Our study will confine itself to *Desolation*, *Felling* (*Tala*), and *Wine Press* (*Lagar*), the three principal books, and to *Tenderness*, which, because it is a collection of children's poems, has special interest. The 1941 *Anthology* reproduces poems already included in all the preceding books.

DESOLATION (*DESOLACIÓN*)

The publication of *Desolation* in 1922, Gabriela Mistral's first book of poems, is one of the important events in the modern history of Hispanic-American poetry. The new voice immediately reveals its originality as it stands out above the chorus of other feminine voices who, according to Federico de Onís, have achieved in that moment of post-modernism, "the full affirmation of their lyrical individuality." [1] Passion, strength, the strange mixture of tenderness and harshness, of delicacy and coarseness,

1 *Antología de la poesía española e hispanoamericana* (Anthology of Spanish and Hispanic American poetry) (Madrid: R.F.E., 1934), p. xviii.

give this voice a unique accent. Her words exercise an irresistible fascination on the reader, leaving in his mouth a bitter aftertaste of blood. After the publication of *Desolation,* Gabriela's fame grew rapidly; a legend began to weave itself around her.

According to the *Introduction (Palabras preliminares),* the book was published thanks to the initiative of Federico de Onís, at that time director of the Hispanic Institute in the United States, and a group of North American Spanish teachers. It was their homage to the great literary and moral value of "a writer of the first rank, in whom the Spanish spirit speaks with new vigor and voice." [2] The publication only reaffirmed the prestige and popularity that Gabriela was enjoying even before the first edition of her works.

Desolation consists of a body of seventy-three poems, grouped under the headings "Life" (*Vida*), "School" (*Escuela*), "For Children" *Infantiles,* "Sorrow" (*Dolor*), and "Nature" (*Naturaleza*), a collection of poetic and poematic prose writings and four cradle songs. The prose writings would merit a separate study. Their themes are the same as those of the poetry: the ideal teacher, the artist and artistic creation, motherhood and children, living beings and materials, the ecstasy of love, the Passion of Christ, death, Beauty, and the Eternal. There are some stories for school, each with a moral, in which the protagonists are not animals, as in the fables, but roses, reeds, the root of the rose bush, the thistle, the pond. Her style recalls the parables of the New Testament. Seeking to avoid direct admonition, the author uses these lovely imaginative fictions to attempt to form the moral conscience of children. One would have to consult these pages written in prose to clarify Gabriela's religious, aesthetic, moral, pedagogical, and social ideas and to determine her literary sources, her readings (the Bible, Tagore, Oriental literature, the *Little Flowers* of San Francisco, Martí, folklore), and the peculiar nature of her sensitivity. Some of her social concerns are evident in the themes of poverty, the seduced woman, illegitimate children, abandoned children, work, class prejudices, self-righteousness, all profoundly tinged with a sense of human solidarity and true Christianity.

2 *Desolación* (Desolation) (1st ed. New York: Hispanic Institute, 1922).

In the "Poems for Mothers" (*Poemas de las madres*) and "Poems of Ecstasy" (*Poemas del éxtasis*), both very beautiful, the poet achieves that fusion of the frankest realism—almost of verbal crudity—with the most delicate poetry: the chaste ardor of a sensuality spiritualized through maternal longing and the religious sense of life that is perhaps the most personal trait of her poetic vision of the world, the one that sets her apart from other American poetesses.

The "Wish" (*Voto*), found on the last page of the book, alludes to anecdotal and biographical elements—her bitterness, the painful past, the finding of hope—and to artistic creation as a catharsis. With the "Wish" she offers her work as if excising a piece of her heart, in order to break free from an already definitive past. She renounces subjectivism, "to stain the song with blood and so relieve oneself." "From the spiritual plateaus I will sing to console men, without ever looking at my heart again" (p. 243). These words are a prelude to the more objective lyricism, the abandonment of the romantic attitude, that is almost literally carried out in *Felling* (*Tala*).

The title *Desolation* is from the first poem of the section "Nature" (*Naturaleza*) and is thus titled because it describes a desolate landscape of mist and fog, a true mental landscape, the projection of a psychological state, which dominates the book and gives the keynote and emphasis to the leading poems.

Eighteen poems appear under the heading "Life" (*Vida*) without forming a unit. A reading of these allows us to enter the world of the poet as we observe her response to the challenge of external events—the killing of Jews in Poland, the death of Amado Nervo, the publication of a book by Alone; her reaction to things—Rodin's "Thinker," the cross of Bistolfi, the Book of Ruth; or to profounder, more subjective experiences—religious faith, love, art itself. The first pages reveal to us her personal accent, her harsh style filled with strong, plastic imagery and realistic, throbbing words, and her primary preoccupations, those that define and give unity to her vision of the world. Pain is an inescapable but redeeming reality; the union with Christ, the longing for motherhood, children, the anguish of creating, and that of dying, will reappear on the pages that follow and in all her later books as poetical constants, but with variations that the passage of time will impose upon them.

"To the Virgin of the Hill" (A *la Virgen de la colina*), "Future" (*Futuro*), and "Serene Words" (*Palabras serenas*) would be better suited to the sections "Sorrow" (*Dolor*) and "Nature" (*Naturaleza*). The first poem is a prayer to the Virgin, analogous to the "Nocturne" (*Nocturno*); the second, with prophetic overtones, communicates the same total desolation as in the "Landscapes of Patagonia" (*Paisajes de la Patagonia*). "Serene Words" repeats in verse the resolutions of the "Wish" (*Voto*) and could be placed in the background.

The reading of these first poems leaves us with an odd impression, like that of a strange, tormented landscape. All the Modernist refinement and subtleties vanish, charred to a crisp by this somber ardor. The words possess the plasticity of clay, and with marvellous ease they keep molding the emotions, the shades of feeling, the heart-rending imprint that reality leaves on the poet's heart. From that heart the verses seem to spring in torrents, barely tempered by reason. They are romantic without rebelliousness or satanism, baroque, yet unpolished in form.

Credo

Creo en mi corazón que cuando canta
sumerje en el Dios hondo el flanco herido
para subir de la piscina viva
como recién nacido.

Creo en mi corazón el que yo exprimo
para teñir el lienzo de la vida
de rojez o palor, y que lo ha hecho
veste encendida.

pp. 35–36.

Creed

I believe in my heart that when
The wounded heart sunk within the depth of God sings
It rises from the pond alive
As if new-born.

I believe in my heart what I wring from myself
To tinge life's canvas
With red or pallid hue, thus clothing it
In luminous garb.

And although the sign of death seems to hover over these poems, we can feel within them the hidden throb of life, of pleasure, of the fondness for palpable beauty, of the impetus to create with which they attempt to elude death's terrible reign. Gabriela's personal adherence to Christ, Christian acceptance of sorrow, love for one's neighbor, the certainty of possessing the gift of song, faith in oneself stand in opposition to the elegiac tone in poems like "In the Ear of Christ" (*Al oído de Cristo*), "The Child Alone" (*El niño solo*), "The Strong Woman" (*La mujer fuerte*), "Creed" (*Credo*). But let not the contradiction deceive us: one must seek the true root of this lyricism in the polarity pleasure-pain, maternity-sterility, hope-desolation, life-death that lends its tautness and heartbreak to the style, that contracts and swells the phrase, that anoints the words now with blood, now with honey. Desolation and tenderness, wine press and felling, the titles of the books, record directly or through symbols the agony of life inherent in this dialectic.

The poems grouped under the headings "School" (*Escuela*) and "For Children" (*Infantiles*) reveal Gabriela's deep interest in children and in the problems of pedagogy. To the strictly poetic values of those verses one must add the validity of their ideas and of the moral or religious lesson they attempt to communicate. The poet considers that the purpose of education is the spiritual formation of the student, the harmonious development of his personality and character. She takes great care to teach and emphasize the primary importance of religious, moral, and aesthetic values and to awaken the student's consciousness of duty, of his relationship to God and creatures, and of the full enjoyment of Beauty. She proposes for him a Christian ethic of love, pardon and service, of respect for all beings, and of confidence in God as a provident and loving father.

She demands of the teacher the virtues of a saint: virility, fortitude, purity, gentleness, sweetness, joyfulness, poverty, submission to pain and death, and inner peace, because she conceives of teaching as a calling and an apostleship, a divine task entrusted to men. With other illustrious teachers of the past, Gabriela believes in the educational power of beauty, and she clothes her teachings in beautiful descriptions, in the playful fantasy of stories, and in the symbolism of the parable. Upon reading these poems we can see that she found in teaching a way of satisfying maternal desires and an outlet for the springs of her stifled tenderness. It was also a way of perpetuating herself by living on in her disciples, as she reveals to us in "The Shining Host" (*El corro luminoso*):

En vano queréis	In vain you try
ahogar mi canción:	To smother my song:
¡un millón de niños	A million children
la canta en un corro	In chorus sing it
debajo del sol!	Beneath the sun!
En vano queréis	In vain you try
quebrarme la estrofa	To break my verse
de tribulación:	Of affliction:
¡el coro la canta	The children sing it
debajo de Dios!	Under God!

p. 49.

Without ever becoming superficial or oversentimentally tasteless, these poems are within the grasp of children's understanding and imagination. They awaken and refine their sensitivity with witty poetic fictions, with the nobility of elevated thoughts. Especially outstanding is "Rounds" (*Rondas*), grouped around the theme of universal harmony. It is a poem in eight parts that reaches its climax when Christ penetrates the chorus, transforming it into a mystical experience. The dance movements, the significance of small gestures, the rich plasticity of description, the beauty of the symbol and the images contain many possibilities for dramatic execution. "Rounds" could be made into a beautiful expressionistic ballet if an intelligent choreographer were to interpret it as a contrast with the medieval dances of death. Through its affirmation of life, love, and peace, the reader perceives the conception of the poem as an attempt to create a true anti-dance macabre:

Los que no danzan	Those Who Do Not Dance
Una nina que es inválida	A crippled child
dijo: "¿Cómo danzo yo?"	Said: "How shall I dance?"
Le dijimos que pusiera	Let your heart dance
a danzar su corazón . . .	We said.
Luego dijo la quebrada:	Then the invalid said:
"¿Cómo cantaría yo?"	"How shall I sing?"
Le dijimos que pusiera	Let your heart sing
a cantar su corazón . . .	We said.

Dijo el pobre cardo muerto: Then spoke the poor dead
"¿Cómo, cómo danzo yo?"   thistle,
Le dijimos: "Pon al viento   "But I, how shall I dance?"
a volar tu corazón . . ."   Let your heart fly to the wind
           We said.
Dijo Dios desde la altura:
"¿Cómo bajo del azul?"   Then God spoke from above
Le dijimos que bajara   "How shall I descend from the
a danzarnos en la luz.   blue?"
           Come dance for us here in the
Todo el valle está danzando   light
en un corro bajo el sol,   We said.
y al que no entra se le ha hecho
tierra, tierra el corazon.   All the valley is dancing
      p. 90. Together under the sun,
           And the heart of him who
            joins us not
           Is turned to dust, to dust.

In the two sections "Sorrow" (*Dolor*) and "Nature" (*Naturaleza*), we find the more impressive poems, those "in which there bleeds a painful past" (p. 243). They provide the internal unity of the book; they justify the title of the book, *Desolation*. The twenty-five poems that follow the first heading speak directly, in the romantic fashion, of love and of pain; the eleven of the second, although they describe landscapes of the furthest point of Chile, reflect as in a mirror intimate loneliness, the hunger for death after the failure of love. The two groups form an inseparable unit.

In "Sorrow" (*Dolor*), the poems are arranged in such a way that they seem to follow the thread of the chronological development of a story from its beginning until its tragic conclusion; the first poem is titled "The Meeting" (*El encuentro*), the last one, "The Bones of the Dead" (*Los huesos de los muertos*). But a careful reading will reveal the presence of another story of love. "The Prayer" (*El ruego*) closes the cycle of the first story; the "Nocturne" (*Norturno*) expresses the crisis of the second, the more decisive one.

But, although the poems in "Sorrow" (*Dolor*) refer to two different experiences, their arrangement in an order that has nothing to do with the strict chronological sequence of events throws the reader off the track and makes him believe that Gabriela is dealing with one only love frustrated by the suicide of the loved one. The poems "Sonnets of Death" (*Sonetos de la muerte*), "Questions" (*Interrogaciones*), "The Obsession" (*La obsesión*), "Songs" (*Coplas*) of page 127, "Eternal Candles" (*Ceras eternas*), "To See Him Again" (*Volverlo a ver*), "The Sentence" (*La condena*), "The Glass" (*El vaso*), "The Prayer" (*El ruego*), and "The Bones of the Dead" (*Los huesos de los muertos*) seem to refer to that particular painful event. "Silent Love" (*El amor que calla*), "Ecstasy" (*Extasis*), "Intimation" (*Intima*), "God Wills It" (*Dios lo quiere*), "Watchful" (*Desvelada*), "Shame" (*Vergüenza*), "Ballad" (*Balada*), "Affliction" (*Tribulación*), "Nocturne" (*Nocturno*), and almost all the poems in the section "Nature" (*Naturaleza*) seem to allude to the second love experienced some years later. This was a profound, ardent experience that opened in the poet's heart a wound whose bleeding traces we can still perceive in *Wine Press* (*Lagar*), her last published book. In "Poem of the Son" (*Poema del hijo*) and "Songs" (*Coplas*) of page 142, the two stories are fused and interlaced.

There is a considerable anecdotal element in these poems, and we run the risk of attaching greater significance to the wealth of biographical allusions than to the pure artistic values. Yet as we read, we cannot help but be amazed at the transformation of living reality into beauty.

Few poets sang of love with more passion, with more wrathful words. How far from the subtleties, the delicate and modest sensitivity of an Elizabeth Barrett Browning or a Christina Rossetti! Here is a possessive, all-absorbing emotion with the force of surf or stormy wind. Here is tenderness smothered by jealousy. Vengeful and rebellious rancor darken the song and wrench from it disturbing resonances; the ecstasy of the flesh shudders with mortal foreboding.

The poems of "Sorrow" (*Dolor*) record the critical moments of the emotional experience [3] sometimes as psychological sensations, sometimes as projections on a rustic landscape that serves

---

3 Let us glance at some titles: "The Meeting" (*El encuentro*), "Ecstasy" (*Extasis*), "Intimation" (*Intima*), "God Wills It" (*Dios lo quiere*), "Watchful" (*Desvelada*), "Affliction" (*Tribulación*), "Sonnets of Death" (*Sonetos de la muerte*), "The Useless Wait" (*La espera inútil*), "To See Him Again" (*Volverlo a ver*), etc.

as its setting. The enamored one wanders through those valleys
and gardens talking with nature's creatures in an intimate dialogue that recalls the accents of the Spouse in the Song of Songs.
Her emotion overflows like an elemental, teluric force, in which
the maternal—almost matriarchal—essence displaces the erotic.
Behind the impassioned tremor we sense the heavy sensuality,
the thirst for earthly happiness that makes the senses tremble,
even though the spirit may be the victor in its struggle for purity
and for perpetuating the transitory.

The poet conceives of love as a demanding, powerful, cunning
divinity that enslaves us and against whom all resistance is futile.
Ruled by its fatal power, she abandons herself to feeling with a
jealous vehemence that has more of hate than of love. Every so
often tenderness, fulfilled pleasure will soften her words: but
the dominant note will always be "all or nothing," the vengeful
fury of a new Medea who does not hesitate to destroy that which
she loves as well as herself.

Dios lo quiere

I

La tierra se hace madrastra
si tu alma vende a mi alma.
Llevan un escalofrío
de tribulación las aguas.
El mundo fué más hermoso
desde que yo te fuí aliada,
cuando junto de un espino
nos quedamos sin palabras,
¡y el amor como el espino
nos traspasó de fragancia!

¡Pero te va a brotar víboras
la tierra si vendes mi alma!
baldías del hijo, rompo
mis rodillas desoladas!
Se apaga Cristo en mi pecho
¡y la puerta de mi casa
quiebra la mano al mendigo
y avienta a la atribulada!

II

Beso que tu boca entregue
a mis oídos alcanza

porque las grutas profundas
me devuelven tus palabras.
El polvo de los senderos
guarda el olor de tus plantas
y oteándolo, como un ciervo,
te sigo por las montañas . . .

A la que tú ames, las nubes
la pintan sobre mi casa.
Vé cual ladrón a besarla
de la tierra en las entrañas;
mas, cuando el rostro le alces,
hallas mi cara con lágrimas.
Dios no quiere que tú bebas
si yo no tiemblo en tu agua.
No consiente que tú duermas
sino en mi trenza ahuecada.

Si te vas, hasta en los musgos
del camino rompes mi alma;
te muerden la sed y el hambre
en todo valle o llanada
y en cualquier país las tardes
con sangre serán mis llagas.

Y destilo de tu lengua
aunque a otra mujer llamaras,
y me clavo como un dejo
de salmuera en tu garganta;
y odies, o cantes, o ansies,
¡por mí solamente clamas!

Si te vas y mueres lejos,
tendrás la mano ahuecada
diez años bajo la tierra
para recibir mis lágrimas,
sintiendo como te tiemblan
las carnes atribuladas,
¡hasta que te espolvoreen
mis huesos sobre la cara!
                    pp. 106–108.

The very earth will reject you
If your soul sells mine.
Within the waters there seethes
The chill of tribulation.
The world was more beautiful
From the time that I was yours,

When together beside a thorn tree
We stood without words,
And love like a thorn
Pierced us with its fragrance!

But snakes will spring from the earth
If you sell my soul;
Barren of child, I crush
My desolate knees.
Christ is stifled within me,
And the door of my house
Breaks the hand of the beggar
And chases the woman in pain.

The kiss you may give another
Rings within my ears
Because the deep caves
Are echoing your words.
The dust of the road
Retains the scent of your steps
And like a deer tracking
I follow you through the mountains . . .

The clouds will paint on my house
The other whom you may love.
Go like a thief to kiss her
In the bowels of the earth;
But when you lift her face
You will find mine tear-filled before you.

God will not let you drink
If I tremble not in the water.
He will not let you sleep
Lest cradled in my tresses.

If you leave you break my soul
On the very moss you tread;
Hunger and thirst will seize you
On every mountain and plain
And in every land the blood-filled days will be my wounds.

And my name slips from your tongue
Though you may call another,
And I will pierce your throat
As with the taste of brine;
And whether you hate, or sing, or long
For me alone you will clamor!

If you leave and distant die,
The hollow of your hand will wait

Ten years beneath the earth
To catch my falling tears,
Feeling the very trembling
Of my afflicted flesh,
Until my bones crumble
To dust upon your face!

The enamored one also speaks with God and attempts to
enlist Him in her cause. When she underlines the spiritual
rather than the physical nature of her emotion, she reveals its
religious sense, the divine spark that illuminates it:

Intima

¡Es un viento de Dios que pasa hendiéndome
el gajo de las carnes volandero!

p. 105.

Intimation

It is a wind of God that passes piercing me
With the fleeting barb of the flesh!

and she warns her beloved that their union is an indissoluble
pact, a decree of the Divinity.

It is not surprising that her song takes the form of prayer in
its moments of fulfillment as well as in those of affliction. Like
Unamuno, she wants to transcend the fleeting aspects of pleasure and worldly ties and conquer death. Her maternal longing
and its antipode, the anguished certainty of dying, drive her to
asceticism. In "Intimation" (*Intima*), she rejects experience of
the flesh that imprisons love in its deathly chains:

Tú no beses mi boca.
Vendrá el instante lleno
de luz menguada, en que estaré sin labios
sobre un mojado suelo.

Y dirás: "La amé, pero no puedo
amarla más, ahora que no aspira
el olor de retamas de mi beso.

p. 104.

You, do not kiss my mouth,
There will come the moment filled

> With dying light, in which I will be without lips
> On a wet ground.

> And you will say: "I loved her once, but can
> No longer love her, now that she cannot breathe
> The genista scent of my kiss.

In "Poem of the Son" (*Poema del hijo*), she escapes from lust
in order to offer her child a pure bed and womb:

> *En las noches, insomne de dicha y de visiones,*
> *la lujuria de fuego no descendió a mi lecho.*
> *Para el que nacería vestido de canciones*
> *yo extendía mi brazo, yo ahuecaba mi pecho.*
>
> p. 139.

> In the nights, sleepless with joy and visions,
> I did not take fiery lust to my bed.
> For the one to be born clothed in songs
> I opened my arms and breast instead.

Sorrow and death are the constant companions of this love,
from its dawn to its sunset, and even in the brief moments of
happiness they cast upon the poetry their somber shadows,
subtle shadings that bind fear to pleasure, anguish to tenderness.

When we enter the inner region of *Desolation* for the first
time, we are surprised to hear a new language of love. Though
still resounding with old echoes, it is free from the refinements
and exquisiteness that literary elegance and urbanity have been
imposing on the expression of love from the days of the Provençal troubadours and Petrarch to the present. The new language free of prudery, reflects rustic realism, the frank manner
with which people who live close to the soil refer to the events
of life and to feelings: a natural simplicity that calls a spade a
spade. The words are direct, concrete, a bit coarse. Their intensity, the ardor of the epithets, the strength of the images
lend purposeful energy and great plasticity to the verses.

Gabriela is not guilty of that immodesty, audacity, and erotic
excess of other women who have sung to love in our America.
Her maternal instinct and her moral and religious sensibility
compel her to be prudent. In her longing for spirituality and
purity she responds, in a very Spanish way, to the problem of
death.

She has struck some critics as excessive, wrathful. Hyperbole is, actually, one of the characteristic traits of her style. Yet there is no doubt that compared to the somewhat decadent preciosity of the Modernists, her voice has the vigor of elemental forces, because she draws emotion directly from the living waters of feeling, from the deep, inner truth of a soul that has not been weakened by the effeminacy of this century.

In 1918 Gabriela went to Punto Arenas on the Straits of Magellan to become director of the school for girls. For two years she stayed in that inhospitable region, in voluntary exile, fleeing from the places in which she had lived the terrible drama of her love. Pursued by cruel memories, desolate, her wounds still fresh, she vented her pain and hunger for death on the new landscape. The poems included in "Nature" (*Naturaleza*), and perhaps the "Songs" (*Coplas*) (p. 142) of "Sorrow" (*Dolor*), were written at this time. They faithfully transmit her brooding mood, that dark longing to immerse herself in despair and solitude.

The description of the landscape is now merely the means by which Gabriela reveals the anguish of her heart. The states at the southernmost tip of Chile have nothing in common with the fertile, luminous beauty of her native Elqui valley, with the fruitful abundance of its orchards, the transparency of its rivers, the warm fragrance of its breezes. Here there is only a white endless plain, howling winds, foggy skies, and a long night, filled with phantoms.

The poet feels alone and abandoned in these places, among people who do not speak her language.

> Los barcos cuyas velas blanquean en el puerto
> vienen de tierras donde no están los que son míos;
> sus hombres de ojos claros no conocen mis ríos
> y traen frutos pálidos, sin la luz de mis huertos.
>
> Y la interrogación que sube a mi garganta
> al mirarlos pasar, me desciende, vencida:
> hablan extrañas lenguas y no la conmovida
> lengua que en tierras de oro mi pobre madre canta.
> Desolation, pp. 149–50.

The ships that fill the port with their sails of white
Come from lands where there are no boats of mine;

They do not know my rivers, these men whose light eyes shine
And they come bearing pale fruit without my orchards' light.

And the rising question that my throat demands
As I watch them pass, vanquished, now retreats:
They speak strange tongues, tongues not so sweet
As the one my mother sings in golden lands.

But at the same time, she initiates a tremendous dialogue with
these beings, a dialogue shaken by fatal omens; and in the
sadness of things and the thousand pained faces of nature about
her, she keeps discovering the projections of her inner world,
the faithful image of her own tragic mask.

The selection of poetic themes reveals the perfect identification between the moral and external landscapes; the images
reveal her conception of sorrow as a bleeding passion similar
to that of Christ, the fixed idea of death as the only, powerful
wellspring of lyricism. The poet watches the snow falling upon
the plain:

> la nieve como el polvo en la huesa;
> miro crecer la niebla como el agonizante.
> > Desolation, p. 150.

> The snow like dust upon the tomb;
> As one dying, I watch the swelling mist.

On the trunk of a dry tree, she notices how

> Arbol muerto

> sube de la herida un purpurino
> musgo, como una estrofa ensangrentada.
> > p. 151.

> Dead Tree

> From the wound there rises a purple
> Moss, like a blood-stained stanza.

As she listens to the tinkle of the rain she wonders if it is
possible to sleep:

> La lluvia lenta

> mientras afuera
> cae, sufriendo, esta agua inerte,

> *esta agua letal hermana*
> *de la Muerte?*
>
> p. 167.

The Slow Rain

> While outside
> There suffering falls this inert water
> This lethal water, sister
> to Death?

And the constant presence of this hidden death gives the landscape its fearful beauty, so removed from the strength, majesty, sweetness, and light of the American scenes in *Felling* (*Tala*) and *Wine Press* (*Lagar*).

The verses of *Desolation* are not "pure." They are deeply rooted in biography; they reveal in all its rawness "the hidden ulcer in which the needle of song is sharpened, becoming lean and taut" (pp. 204 and 243). With strong realism, she treats the *res psicologica* in as direct, frank, and stark a manner as she treats, on other occasions, her ecstatic rapture over things: bread, salt, air, water, doves.

We have here in verse a kind of "tragic sense of love." The song is born of pain and blood with the hoarse accents of the elegies of Job and the taste of ashes of Ecclesiastes. It is torn by tremendous forces of life and death. Passion, like the burning wind of the desert, shakes it and leaves in one's mouth the bitter sediment of disillusion. Now there is the stammering of love's ecstasy, of maternal tenderness, the joy of beauty; now the cry of the mortal anguish of the flesh as it demands eternity. Her desolate outcry rises in the presence of God; she seeks Christ, the Redeemer, and pleads with Him for rest and peace. And the lyricism surges forth from the wounded heart in a torrent of ardent words, at times prayer, at times shrill cry. One should not look for intellectual poetry on these pages; this is the voice whose essence is passion and instinct. Its sweeping force does not permit exquisite refinement of form and language.

It would not be just to attribute the irregularity of the verses in *Desolation* exclusively to the poet's lack of ability in handling metric forms. Gabriela was a very conscientious artist, concerned with the perfection of her work. Her manuscripts reveal numerous erasures and substitutions of words, the reworking of entire lines, and changes of rhythm. Every so often the drive to improve the text almost goes to vicious extremes: at such times the improved version loses much of its original freshness and intensity. A comparison of a poem's different versions would throw a great deal of light on Gabriela's "poetics" and on her way of handling language.

In *Desolation* one finds poems of perfect form and irregular, unpolished ones side by side. We maintain that she is more concerned with the precision and expressiveness of the word than with the meter of the verse lines. This book contains a great variety of stanzas—sonnets, terzets, quatrains, the five-line stanza, sextains, ballads, and short ballads—all handled with great freedom, without concern for the conventional molds. The poet avails herself of the Modernist inheritance and gives preference to the alexandrine, the hendecasyllable line, and the nine-syllable line. She treats the sonnet form with great ease without limiting herself to Renaissance patterns. In the poem "The Oak" (*La encina*) (pp. 46–47), there is an individual innovation with the addition of a sextain to the second sonnet, which serves as a kind of chorus.

The arrangement of the rhymes does not follow the classical order; Gabriela introduces new schemes. Quite often her consonants are imperfect or they are mixed with assonances. There is an abundance of quatrains in about fifteen different combinations that join together lines of fourteen, eleven, nine, eight, seven, and six syllables. Besides the orthodox ballad and short ballad she writes ballads of ten and nine-syllable lines. The use of this last meter—that of the nine-syllable line—interests us because it becomes the preferred verse line in her later books. It is a line that has been used in Spanish poetry since the thirteenth century. Rubén Darió revived it and again made it fashionable among the Modernists. Gabriela appropriates it for herself; there is something in this rhythm that is well suited to the slow, muted inflection of her voice, to the melodic curve of her customary, individual intonation. Those who have heard her recite her own poems know that on her lips they sound like the hushed murmur of prayers or psalms.

Also taken from Modernism are the overflow lines and stanzas and the placing of unaccented words—prepositions or conjunctions—at the end of the rhyme. It is hardly a felicitous innovation, barely used in our poetry, but it can be employed to achieve certain effects of harshness. The *ligato* of the overflow likewise mutes the sharp vivacity of the phrase's musical movement.

There is in Gabriela's poetry a general tendency to isosyllabism, to monotonous stretches of equal lines, with the serious danger of falling into singsong. Such a propensity is more evident in the books that follow *Desolation*. Here, on the contrary, we note a large variety of anasyllabic combinations, in addition to some lines that stand alone. These help to break the uniform beat of the rhymes. Her short-metered poems have a subtle charm, a happy melody that recalls the freshness of folk poetry. It is the air of rounds, ballads, couplets, and lullabies, and its melodic beauty heightens the delicate tremor of the lyricism. The poem "Ballad" (*Balada*) (p. 112) stands out from this group as a small masterpiece.

TENDERNESS (TERNURA)

Gabriela's second book, *Tenderness*,[4] of which there are already four editions, is a collection of all her children's poems up to 1945. The last edition reproduces those published in the three preceding editions, in the first two of *Desolation*, those from *Felling* (*Tala*), and a score of new poems. The book opens with a dedication to her mother and sister, Emelina, both of whom exercised so much influence on Gabriela's spiritual formation and on her choice of teaching as a career. *Tenderness* contains seven sections: "Lullabies" (*Canciones de cuna*), "Rounds" (*Rondas*), "The Raving Woman" (*La desvariadora*), "Tricks" (*Jugarretas*), "Story-World" (*Cuenta-Mundo*), "Almost for School" (*Casi escolares*), "Stories" (*Cuentos*), and a "Colophon by Way of Explanation" (*Colofon con cara de excusa*). The "Colofón," datelined Petropolis, Brazil, is of great interest for the critical evaluation of Mistral's children's poetry

4 Gabriela Mistral, *Ternura* (4th ed., Buenos Aires: Espasa-Calpe, 1945).

and very useful in sketching an intellectual and moral portrait of the poet. Most of this commentary is devoted to the presentation of a theory on the origin of cradle songs, the explanation of the scarcity of such songs in American lands, and the reasons for their present decline. She sees the most important factor as "the decline of physical motherhood, not only the reduction in the number of children but the refusal of many woman to bear children or to be the milking fig tree of stories. The woman who has never nursed, who does not feel the weight of her child against her body, who never puts anyone to sleep day or night, how can she possibly hum a *berceuse*" (p. 185)? The definition of the lullaby as "the dialogue that takes place each day and night between the mother and her soul, her child and the Gea, visible during the day and audible at night" (p. 184) strikes us as the best, the most precise, and the most profound of any we have heard.

The titles of the different sections correspond to those in former editions, with the exception of "Tricks" (*Jugarretas*), which in *Felling* (*Tala*) was called "Reward" (*Albricia*), and "Almost for School" (*Casi escolares*), which was called "For Children" (*Infantiles*) in *Desolation*. In both cases, the change indicates the desire to establish a more precise correlation between the title and the content and tone of the poems appearing under those titles. *The Raving Woman* (*La desvariadora*), which mostly contains new poems, is also a highly appropriate name because all these poems refer to fantasies and exaggerations born of the obsession with motherhood.

Some poems are not very suitably grouped. "Mexican Child" (*Niño mexicano*) is not truly a lullaby; in "The Little Box of Olinalá" (*La cajita de Olinalá*), there is no raving by a delighted mother; "Little Red Riding Hood" (*Caperucita Roja*) retells the well-known story, highlighting its ferocious aspect, and has nothing in common with the charming and original fantasies of "Mother Pomegranate" (*La madre granada*) and "The Pine with Pine Cones" (*El piño de piñas*); it seems to be the least pedagogical, the least suited to a child's sensibilities. "Caress" (*Caricia*), "Sweetness" (*Dulzura*), "Little Worker" (*Obrerito*) express pure filial tenderness without the didactic or moralizing purposes of the other poems in this same section.

The title, *Tenderness,* is well suited to the general character of the book and to the principal emotion that is the source of its poetry. All the poems sing to the pleasure of motherhood, the miracle of having a child, the charm of little animals, the loving understanding between the earth and its creatures. After the tremendous passionate, sensual energy of *Desolation,* this second work reveals to us the powerful vitality, the hunger for happiness, "the spiritualization of voluptuousness which is tenderness," [5] the other poles of the poet's spirit.

Gabriela pours forth into these poems her longing to transcend the ephemeral aspects of passion through motherhood, to seek the eternal in the transitory. It is significant that in "Song of Death" (*Canción de la Muerte*) she calls death the "Counter-mother of the world" (*Contra-Madre del Mundo*) (*Tenderness,* p. 54).

The themes of *Tenderness* duplicate almost all the major motifs of her poetry: maternal love, its pleasures, enchantments, fears, fantasies; the child, his games and legends; the earth (nature, landscape, heavens, constellations); matter (animals, vegetables, minerals, things made by man); toil; America, sleep, death, peace, cosmic harmony, Jesus Christ, God the Father. The poetic development of such rich, varied material keeps these poems free from monotony, trivia, foolishness, and the shoddy prosiness, too often found in this genre. Gabriela is not guilty of becoming artificially child-like, of abandoning the adult point of view, nor of using the silly language that adults presumptuously attribute to children. She makes use of that reserve of unspoiled childhood latent in the spirit of all great poets, and she has attempted (so she tells us in the Colofón) to follow the model of European children's folklore (Spanish, Provençal, Italian) and of general folklore itself, "in search of childlike language, attempting to fathom the clear, profound mystery of its expression." Above all, she has loved and respected the memory of children (p. 190), striving to fathom the secrets of their souls, their imaginative and creative energy, the intensity of their attention. She knows very well that "the singer or balladeer for little ones, the chanter of their dwarf-like

5 Jorge Mañach, *Gabriela: alma y tierra. En Gabriela Mistral,* Vida y *obra,* Bibliografía. Antología. (New York: Hispanic Institute, 1936), p. 7.

cathedral, the master of their songs is not just created, but comes slowly along his starry way, and no one can hasten him along" (p. 189).

From the beginning of her literary career she had worked on this difficult genre, and perhaps no other American poet— except the Martí of *Ismaelillo*—has achieved more beautiful, authentic, and convincing results. All her children's poems have the same depth and intensity of conception and emotion as her adult poetry, qualities that admirably frame the very mischief, malice, playful grace of rhythm, and intent of the verses of childhood. Nothing is spontaneous in these poems: even the most fleeting glance discloses the artistic deliberation evident at each step. Gabriela's comments in "Colofón" indisputably corroborate this observation. The poet has stated for herself all the problems of this genre and has made a strenuous effort to solve them; she is fully aware of her successes and failures. Not the least of the difficulties involved is the struggle with language, the desire to overcome what she calls "verbal hybridization." "Speech," she affirms, "is, after the soul, our second possession and perhaps we have no other possession in this world. Let the one who experiments with it and knows he is experimenting rework it as he pleases" (pp. 189–90).

The result of this vigilance is the precedence of the intellectual note over the sentimental and instructive in these poems: that which is exclusively due to "art" is more evident here than in *Desolation*. By saying this we do not detract from the poetic values of *Ternura*. Quite the contrary. The Cuban Jorge Mañach has already made a decisive and just evaluation.

This art of speaking to childhood is one which only those who have a very deep sense of the spiritual and the concrete can master. The fusion of tremulousness with plasticity, of the malice of beautiful expression with the innocence of the emotion—what a faultless achievement in the pages of *Ternura*! [p. 8]

The wide publication of the lullabies, rounds, and games in this book is evidence of their success. Gabriela has followed the traditional Spanish rhythms closely, giving preference to the ballad form. Besides this form, there also appear the heptasyllabic and hexasyllabic short ballads, the unfinished *seguidilla*, short songs and rondelet-like refrains. There is an abundance of similar combinations based on the nine-syllable line, a meter that is very common in her poetry. The monotony and regularity of the rhyme in these forms is broken at times by a certain harshness and dissonance, by the sudden insertion of a long line or a shorter one, or by an unexpected change of rhyme. The repetition of phrases and lines and the parallelism of their internal structure creates an effect similar to the humming and rhythm of rounds. Gabriela's verse line, very rarely melodic, imparts a sensation of muffled, rending, insistent murmur. On occasions, however, it achieves a winged lightness, a heightened vivacity, and is filled with folkloric grace and freedom.

If we were to study these poems in the chronological order in which they were written, we would observe the change within them wrought by the passage of time. Those published in *Desolation* greatly resemble traditional lullabies and rounds. The very immediate influence of Spanish folklore is confirmed at every step. The musical forms do not offer any variety. Those found in the section "For Children" (*Infantiles*) seem to have been written for possible classroom use; and this is precisely the use to which they have been put. Almost all of them embody a moral teaching or attempt to develop in the student specific attitudes, inclinations, and sentiments: love for nature and country, respect for animals, attention to the miracles of creation, brotherly union, the encouragement of fantasy and of the aesthetic sense. We perceive traces of the Old Testament and of the *Little Flowers* of St. Francis. Franciscan love for all beings acts as a common denominator in all the poems.

The children's poems of *Felling* (*Tala*) are already completely different. The poet has freed herself from her models and attempts original subject matter and rhythms; she has rid herself completely of academic concerns. The lullabies, more elaborate, more correct, more interesting from the artistic point of view, have lost something of the freshness and naturalness of the first ones. The other poems, no longer concerned with pedagogy, gain in malice, in imaginative intoxication, in playfulness. "The One-Armed" (*La manca*), "The Little Straw" (*La pajita*), "The Parrot" (*El papagayo*) demonstrate the extent to which the poet has managed to approach the child's soul, to put us in his place and capture his way of seeing and feeling reality.

The delicious stories "Mother Pomegranate" (*La madre granada*) and "The Pine with Pine Cones" (*El piño de piñas*), a series of somewhat ironic personifications and enchanting, suggestive images—some already very intellectualized—share a strong plasticity that could be compared to the absurd fantasies of Walt Disney.

But the more recent poems, those that incorporate the American theme into the children's genre, appear more terse in their treatment, somewhat forced, perhaps too literary. Some of their details remind us of Góngora and García Lorca. "The Arrorró of Elqui" (*El arrorró elquino*), "Quechua Song" (*La canción quechua*), "Patagonian Lullaby" (*Arrullo patagón*), "The Round of the Ecuadorian Ceiba Tree" (*Ronda de la ceiba equatoriana*) are examples of her effort to create American children's songs against a background of regional local color; her vocabulary in these poems is a mixture of regional and indigenous expressions, with allusions to the flora, the fauna, the beliefs, superstitutions and the Indian culture of these lands.

Still more elaborate are the "Song of Virgo" (*Canción de Virgo*) and the "Song of Taurus" (*Canción de Taurus*), which create a series of myths of stellar motherhood. The poet seems to attribute a maternal sense to the entire universe, not only to the earth. It is curious that there is never any mention made of the father in these poems—an allusion that, on the other hand, is usually recurrent in folk lullabies. In these poems, the mother, or the thousand mothers, give themselves completely to the sweet task of lulling their children to sleep. In this intimate colloquy—actually almost a monologue—the mother tells her child about the world; she unburdens herself of her most secret worries, sorrows, and forebodings. In the rhythmic sway of the lullaby, there is a gradual tightening of the ties that bind the creative love of God—the only Father who has access to this closed circle—to the love of the earth for its little creatures. In several lullabies and rounds we witness this gradual expansion, like the widening of concentric circles, that starts with the mother's song and gradually grows until it embraces the totality of the cosmos and God himself, "the only love that moves the Sun and the other stars." Motherhood has a double significance for Gabriela: it is part of the divine because it is a joyous crea-

tion; it attains the eternal because it scoffs at death and spiritualizes the fleeting pleasures of the flesh.

> *¡es un viento de Dios que pasa hendiéndome*
> *el gajo de las carnes, volandero!*

> It is a wind of God that passes, piercing me
> With the fleeting barb of the flesh!

FELLING (TALA)

Publication. For sixteen years after *Desolation* no new book
by Gabriela Mistral appeared, although during that time she
was writing and publishing in the newspapers of Hispanic
America. Contrary to what some thought, her voice had not
been silent. Proof of the poet's incessant work, of her sure steps
toward the fulfillment of her art can be found throughout those
years in the pages of the newspapers, *El Repertorio Americano*
of Costa Rica, *El Mercurio* of Chile, *El Tiempo* of Colombia,
La Nación and *Crítica* of Buenos Aires, the journals *Atenea,*
Sur, and *Bimestre Cubana,* besides what was published in Spain
and translated in the dailies of France, Portugal, and Brazil.

Felling was published in 1938,[6] but to understand it completely one must bear in mind that it is a compilation of poems
written at different times and under diverse circumstances. In
the span of time from 1922 to 1938 Gabriela's life and art had
undergone profound changes. Like a thermometer, her poetry
recorded the variations. It would be easy enough to fix the date
of almost all the poems in *Felling;* we have witnessed the
writing of most of them. But such a fixing of dates would be
peripheral to the point we wish to make here, and so for the
moment we shall forego this. The alert reader will easily be
able to distinguish the older poems from the more recent ones.
The difference is evident in the language of some and the tone
of others.

Like its predecessor, *Felling* was born of a particular circum-
stance; without it, the poems might still be dispersed throughout the perishable pages of newspapers. It was born of a gesture
of love, a generous act of charity toward the children of Spain,

6 *Tala* (Buenos Aires: Sur, 1938).

innocent beings scattered to the four corners of the earth during
the years of the second war for independence. Gabriela was
ashamed and astonished at the indifference of the Americas,
for she believed they should have been the first to receive
those children of their blood.

The manuscript of *Felling* was offered as a gift to the children of Spain, Catalonians, Castilians, and Basques, uprooted
from their homes by the foreign invasion. The proceeds of its
sale went to the children's camp of Pedralbes, and on two
occasions the funds helped alleviate the poverty in the concen-
tration camps of France. The prestige of the poet guaranteed
very successful sales and a high profit. There is no need to
enhance the nature of this gift. With *Felling* Gabriela re-
nounced what could have formed a basis for her economic
security. But she did it happily, as one who fulfills a duty.

Dedication and Title. The work is dedicated to "Palma
Guillén and, in her, the piety of the Mexican woman." The
fruits of the book's publication and this dedication consolidated
and liquidated the debt of the Americas toward the Spanish children as well as the poet's personal debt to a land of noble
women who had made her welcome during the days of her
collaboration with Vasconcelos in Mexico. Palma Guillén, with
her extraordinary heart and keen spirit, fully embodied the
compassion of Mexican women. By a significant coincidence,
Mexico was the only American land whose moral attitude
toward the dilemma of the helpless Spanish children was an
exception to the indifference that had so shocked Gabriela.

The title of the work, *Felling*, the felling of trees, establishes
the nature of its content, the poet's subjective relationship to
her verses and, in a certain way, the gesture of the gift offering.
These poems are offered as fragments cut from the living body,
which still retains the stumps and roots. The act of creation is
seen as a release; and deep within the mutilated trunks there
remains the latent promise of a new forest.

Notes. At the end of the book there are some notes in which
the poet defends her right to say something to reflect upon her
own work and to help the reader, "like an elf that suddenly
appears before him and walks with him along the road a bit."
In the notes she explains the title, the history, and content of

some poems; she justifies the spontaneous use of internal rhymes
and some cases of omitted rhymes; she gives reasons for her
use of archaic expressions and popular neologisms and collo-
quialisms: she considers the epic genre and the hymn at great
length, finding them forms suitable to the singing of American
nature, and she defines the class of poems she calls "messages"
(*recados*).

There are only a few notes of personal confession: the religious crisis provoked by her mother's death; the rediscovery
of hope; the negative appraisal of sorrow. There are two
recollections of childhood in the Elqui valley: the park of don
Adolfo Iribarren in Montegrande, which inspired her poem
"We Were All Going To Be Queens" (*Todas íbamos a ser
reinas*) and the game of "joy" (*albricias*), which serves as a
title for one of the children's sections. When she speaks of
the *recados*, she confesses that on several occasions she wrote
letters in a genre halfway between verse and prose, a somewhat
plebeian, playful genre that she relegated to pages outside the
book. The *recados* were included because of feminine whim,
because they were framed in the more personal, more usual
tone, the rural inflection with which she had lived and with
which she would die.

There are many more notes on poetry and language. Linguistic
problems had been a constant concern of Gabriela Mistral. It
would be worthwhile compiling in book form her ideas and
observations, her experience in the manipulation of language.
We who have closely observed her create and elaborate poems
and prose know how much care she gave to her words and expressions. We also know with what care she corrected and
reworked what she had written, as she searched for an expression
that would come close to the spoken language, that would have
precision and the warmth of life and would correspond exactly
to the mental image.

In the notes of *Felling* Gabriela defends the use of archaic
expressions in her poetry on the basis of the naturalness and
frequency of their use in the rural speech of the Americas. The
rural speech of the Elqui valley was the source for her archaisms.
Some critics mistakenly believed that they were born of her
reading of the Spanish classical writers of the sixteenth century.

Of course, those Elquian archaisms are mostly of Spanish origin.

These observations reveal her fond, somewhat conservative attitude toward her native region and her preference for the spoken language. Her vocabulary obeys the inclinations of feelings rather than logic. On the other hand, the writer's linguistic conscience impels her to use plain, easy archaisms consistent with her efficacy of expression.

She also justifies the borrowing of foreign words—as long as they are neo-Latin—in cases of logical or emotional need. If she gives to one section of her book the Portuguese title, *Saudade*, it is because she is aware that the Castilian word *soledad* does not have a completely equivalent meaning in the Americas. Again, her keen linguistic consciousness comes to the fore. The French, Italian, and Portuguese words are easily assimilated by the Spanish because they all have the same Latin roots.

She writes *Efigenia* for *Ifigenia* because the name is pronounced that way in Elqui, and *albricia* for *albricias* because the former spelling endows the word with the unique meaning of "reward," "luck," or "gift." In both cases, the poet prefers the truly popular and oral forms to the learned ones. She believes that the differentiation of the initial "I" in *Ifigenia* is easier for the tongue and more pleasing to the ear. The singular of *albricia* is employed for two reasons: out of sentimental recollection of childhood experiences and because of the logical correspondence the poet feels should exist between the idea contained within the word and its morphology. In these comments on language, Gabriela reveals to us her disdain for overcorrectness, pedantry, or deliberate purity. And she praises the people as "the best verbal creatures God has produced."

A similar preoccupation with spontaneity is seen in the notes on the technique of verse; there is an identical respect for the intuitions of the people and of children, whom she calls "complete poetic creatures." Her disdain is aimed at rhetorical sound and at the advocates of rhythmic monotony.

She observes that there are few rhymes at the beginning of the composition and that within a short while they begin to descend like heavy rain intruding into the verse line itself.

At that moment, the internal rhyme becomes natural, and avoiding it could seem to be artificial rebellion. On the other hand, the omission of rhymes helps avoid a singsong pattern. The antepenultimate rhymes seem to her neither "necessary nor useless." She describes her own ear as "rough and careless."

But surely these notes on rhyme contradict such a disdainful self-appraisal. They indicate how important the poet considers auditory sensitivity and rhythmic stimulus. On several occasions we heard her say that most of her poems had been born of an inner rhythm that very gradually took on form and substance. The poetic content followed later, as a consequence. In her note on the *recados*, she adds that she usually writes "feeling all about me the flutter of a rhythm and some rhymes of the kind I call intrusive."

In this way we can explain the frequency—almost the danger —of the regular and insistent rhythms in Gabriela's poetry: a slow flowing of monotonous lines linked by alternating rhymes. The sound evokes the grave measures of the ancient ballad, or the calm current of that river that sings in the poet's veins:

Cosas

Un río suena siempre cerca.
Ha cuarenta años que lo siento.
Es canturía de mi sangre
O bien un ritmo que me dieron.

O el río de Elqui de mi infancia
que me repecho y me vadeo.
Nunca lo pierdo; pecho a pecho,
como dos niños, nos tenemos.
5th part, *Tala*, pp. 137–38.

Things

Beside me a river always sings.
I've felt it now for forty years.
It is the music of my blood
Or yet a rhythm born to me.

Or the river Elqui of my childhood
Whether up the hill or fording.
I never lose it; heart to heart,
Like two children, embraced.

In this book Gabriela attempts the hymn in major key. In America, she says, there has been an overabundance of poetry concerned with trivialities; the minor key is already becoming cloying. There is needed a full-bodied voice to sing to the sun, the mountains, to indigenous monuments, a voice that "has the courage to approach those formidable materials." The hymn and the theme of American nature were initiated by Rubén Darío with his "Triumphal March" (*Marcha triunfal*) and his "Song to Roosevelt" (*Canto a Roosevelt*). Gabriela's two hymns attempt to stimulate in young people the desire to complete the task. They renew the current of Americanism, but in the continental rather than national sense of the word, and with a deeper consciousness of race and soil. The poet laments the fact that we have limited the poetry of landscape to descriptions of individualized details. The Andes, the sun, the Orinoco seem to her to be more worthy of song than butterflies and humming birds. Her telluric and cosmic sensitivity demands that attention be paid to the elements, to the primary forces of nature. And the poetic accent should correspond to the majesty of such themes. For this reason she predicts a return to the martial odes.

Change.   The poetic world of *Felling* differs radically from that of *Desolation*. Going from one to other is like going from the Old Testament to the Gospels. Or it may be likened to entering the illuminating state of mysticism after leaving behind the asperities of asceticism. The entire atmosphere has changed; happiness modulates the style. In *Felling* there speaks the spirit that has controlled the flesh. Her voice retains its passionate rapture, but the structural rhythm now flows in peaceful measures, though it is still intense. At certain moments hope is raised to the high-pitched, joyous heights of ecstasy. The poem "Grace" (*La Gracia*), which strikes us as being the lyrical peak of her work and its culmination, captures the essence of this spiritual moment in words of intense conciseness. Some lines echo accents heard in Saint John of the Cross.

Pareció lirio	It seemed a lily
o pez-espada.	Or sword fish to me,
Subió los aires	It scaled the airs
hondeada,	Pulling free,
de cielo abierto	Devoured by the open sky

devorada,	Hungrily,
y en un momento	And in a moment
fué nonada.	A mere speck to see.
Quedé temblando	I stood trembling
en la quebrada.	In the ravine,
¡Albricia mía!	Oh, joy of mine!
¡arrebatada!	Torn from me!
Felling, p. 55.	

Content   The first section of *Felling,* "Death of My Mother" (*Muerte de mi Madre*), establishes the continuity between this book and its predecessor. "The Flight" (*La fuga*), the "Nocturnes of Consummation" (*Nocturnos de la consumación*), "The Defeat" (*La derrota*), and "Old Weavers" (*Tejedores viejos*) prolong the religious crisis already noted in the aforementioned "Nocturne." "Mad Litanies" (*Locas letanías*) and "Nocturne of the Descent" (*Nocturno del descendimiento*), on the other hand, manifest the return to hope, the true entry into a new moral climate. The second of these poems is reminiscent of some passages from "The Christ of Velázquez" (*El Cristo de Velázquez*) by Unamuno; the first sings with the joy of faith in resurrection. Pain at her mother's death has transformed itself into the certainty of a future life in the peace of Christ. We know that this change occurred following the reading of Henri Bergson's *Les deux sources de la religion et de la morale.* The chapter in which Bergson studies Christian mysticism moved the poet deeply and started her longing and searching for grace.

The second part, "Hallucination" (*Alucinación*), contains recollections, dreams, and visions like "Paradise" (*Paraíso*) and "Midnight" (*La medianoche*). "Tales of the Madwoman" (*Historias de loca*) merit special attention. Their dominant characteristic is fantasy; the first tale imagines the world as it was before the birth of death and records the terrible effects upon everything of this newly-born death. In the second poem, the nature of poetry is likened to a "flower of the air"; the third tells of the spiritual liberation of the soul as it divests itself of the body, that shadow that had always chained it to the law of time; the fourth relates a dream-like experience. These four poems gather together all the major themes of Gabriela Mistral's latest poetry: death, the absolute, poetry, dreams. They are not tales of a madwoman; on the contrary, they contain some of the poet's deepest, most elaborate thoughts.

The section called "Matter" (*Materias*) presents us with another kind of poetic experience: the rapture she feels as she looks at things that suddenly seem to reveal the hidden essence of their being. Beneath our gaze one day, bread, salt, water, air take on values they never had before. It is a rediscovery filled with surprises, a kind of mystical union with reality. For a moment the poet senses the divine presence in things and loses herself in fascinated contemplation.

Beneath the heading "America" (*América*) are joined together eulogies, landscapes, and memories of our continent; the tropical sun, the Andes, the hills and palm groves of Puerto Rico, the Panamanian dance *tamborito*; she sings to the Americas with the fervor of one in love. She sees the sun and the mountain range as unifying factors in the Americas and envisions the United States of the South both as a political reality and a cultural unit based on the restoration of the indigenous past to the present. Gabriela's Americanism goes beyond national frontiers and embraces in the same loving gesture the Mexican child, the sweet earth of Puerto Rico, the pagan spell of the *tamborito*.

The language in all these poems is enthusiastic and passionate. The two Hymns have the hyperbolic accents of a litany; the vision of Puerto Rico is captured with maternal tenderness; the description of the Mexican cornfield and of Mexican men has the power of a stone relief or the ritualistic rhythm of a Diego Rivera fresco.

Las mesas del maíz	The tables of corn
quieren que yo me acuerde.	Want me to remember.
El corro está mirándome	The group gazes at me
fugaz y eternamente.	Fleetingly and eternal.
Los sentados son órganos,	The seated men are organ
Las sentadas magueyes.	cactus,
Delante de mi pecho	The women maguey.
La mazorcada tienden.	Before my breast
De la voz y los modos	They spread the ears of corn.
gracia tolteca llueve.	Their voices and their manner
La casta come lento,	Bespeak their Toltec grace.
como el venado bebe.	The clan eats slowly,
Dorados son el hombre,	As the young deer drinks.

el bocado, el aceite,   Golden are the men,
y en sesgo de ave pasan   The food, the oil,
las jícaras alegres.   And like the graceful sweep
Otra vez me tuvieron   of birds
éstos que aquí me tiene,   The happy chocolate cups are
y el corro, de lo eterno,   passed.
parece que espejee . . .   Once before they held me
. . . .   They who hold me now,
El pecho del maíz   This group which seems to
su fervor lo retiene.   shine,
El ojo del maíz,   With the light of eternity . . .
tiene el abismo breve.   . . . .
Su obsidiana se funde   The breast of the corn
como una contra-nieve.   Retains its warmth.
El habla del maíz   The eye of the corn,
en valva y valva envuelve.   Bares a shallow abyss.
Ley Vieja del maíz,   Its obsidian melts
caída no perece,   As a counter-snow.
y el hombre del maíz   The tongue of the corn
se juega, no se pierde.   In sheath upon sheath
    Felling, pp. 108–10.   enclosed.
                                         Ancient law of the corn,
                                         Which fallen, does not
                                             perish,
                                         And the man of the corn
                                         Moves with it, never lost.

In Nostalgia (*Saudade*) the poet gathers together poems dealing with longing, visions of childhood, children's gestures, lost and longed for things. The poems on the theme of love, grouped together in the section "The Dead Wave" (*La ola muerta*), seem to have been written during much earlier periods of time and do not form a homogeneous entity. "Wall" (*Muro*) and "Old Lion" (*Viejo león*) seem to be the oldest. "Absence" (*Ausencia*) and "Good-bye" (*Adiós*) follow them chronologically. "Day" (*Día*) and "Ill" (*Enfermo*) are the most recent. The tone of these last poems and even that of "Good-bye" (*Adiós*) indicates such a certainty in the truth of love, in its ability to triumph over material obstacles, in its abundant happiness that it is impossible to relate them to those tremendous, desolate poems of the year 1922. The more recent emotional experience seems a much happier one. "Old Lion" (*Viejo león*) does not fit into this body of work.

The section entitled "Creatures" (*Criaturas*) should logically follow "Matter" (*Materias*). It consists of a series of portraits and evocations of dead and living people, several eulogies, and some poems that underscore the impact of all divine and human realities upon the poet. The last poem, "Doves" (*Palomas*), the only one that describes a bird, would be better suited to the group of poems within "Matter," because it is similar in mood to poems like "Salt" (*Sal*) and "Bread" (*Pan*) as it speaks of the ecstatic rediscovery of familiar objects.

The "Lullabies" (*Canciones de cuna*), the precursors of which can be found in *Desolation*, are songs of the mother lulling her child to sleep with tender words. In "The Story World" (*La cuenta-mundo*), the same mother speaks to her son of the world around him in graceful and profound metaphors. In both sections there is evident a sense of identification and familiarity with the earth. Everything is personified, and both living creatures and inanimate things are bound together in a Franciscan brotherhood of love. There is an unmistakable religious accent and note of thanksgiving in the happiness of these beings and the sense of wonder they engender.

The children's poems appear in the next to last section of *Felling*. The language used in these little poems proves to be the most fitting for children's poetry. Untrammelled imagination, the marvelous or absurd anecdote, affectionate language, the regular repetitions and rhythms that childhood loves so much and that are so natural to its poetry are all to be found in these verses. The poet has returned to childhood through some surprising miracle and has managed to reproduce with utmost fidelity the poetic and linguistic sense of this first moment of life. The fact that this section is titled *Albricia*, that is, "reward," seems doubly apt: playing at the game of *las albricias*, she has come upon the hidden treasure of authentic children's poetry, so scarce in Spanish literature.

She closes the work with the "Messages" (*Recados*), a kind of poetic letter that sometimes carries a request and sometimes praises some creature. These letters roam the earth, from Mexico to Chile, from Catalonia to the Antilles, from Castile to Argentina. They are letters from a woman for women, written with unaffected ease, in a gay, metaphoric language. In them the poet pays tribute to friendship and comments on contemporary events in an indirect way. Even her deepest preoccupations exaggerate the tart and playful note.

The sections could be arranged in a more logical sequence, on the basis of the psychological content and mood of each one. For example: "Death of My Mother" (*Muerte de mi madre*), "The Dead Wave" (*La ola muerta*), "Nostalgia" (*Saudade*), "Hallucination" (*Alucinación*), "Tales of a Madwoman" (*Historias de loca*), "Matter" (*Materias*), "Creatures" (*Criaturas*), "Messages" (*Recados*), "America," "Joy" (*Albricias*), "Lullabies" (*Canciones de cuna*), and "The Story-World" (*La cuentamundo*).

These twelve parts could be reduced to five fundamental themes: religious crisis, the evocation of the past, self-confession, children, and beings and nature. This is a profoundly lyrical poetry, a much more objectivized lyricism than that of *Desolation*. The poet sings of herself, of her "I," and offers each poem as a part of her innermost being. Even when she speaks of a creature or a thing she is only underscoring her electrically alive relationship to all things in the world. However, she is never absolutely objective: in the description or praise of another, there is an almost mystical effusion of the "I." In addition, the verses for children give full rein to maternal longing, one of the strongest mainsprings of Gabriela's inner and outer behavior. A tremendous longing for God dominates this intensely personal lyricism. God is implicitly present in all the verses of *Felling*, as the single theme, as the most genuine and constant preoccupation. Love for things, obliviousness to her own happiness, her very humble confession of errors form the path by which the poet seeks to reach the Supreme Being. The grace of Christ, like the archangel, walks with her along the way.

Meter The form of this book is of extraordinary interest. There is one group of poems written in stanzas of unequal length, with neither a fixed metric pattern nor rhyme. In these stanzas there is a completely arbitrary combination of free verse lines of eleven, twelve, thirteen, and fourteen syllables. "The Drink" (*La copa*), "Midnight" (*La medianoche*), "Paradise" (*Paraíso*), "Wall" (*Muro*), "Confession" (*La confesión*), and the messages "Birth" (*Nacimiento*), "To Lolita Arriaga" (*A Lolita Arriaga*), and "To Rafael Ortega, in Castile" (*A Rafael*

Ortega, en Castilla) belong to this group. In all of these the similarity of form derives from an identity of tone and poetic manner. We do not think it speculation to affirm that these poems may have been written at the same period of time, and much earlier than the year 1933.

Apart from these, we observe in the rest of the book the following: The abundance of verse lines of seven, eight, nine, and ten syllables, with a marked predominance of the nine-syllable line. The inclination toward isosyllabism does not prevent a shorter or longer line from capriciously breaking the regularity from time to time. There are some combinations of eleven- and seven-syllable lines, of seven- and five-syllable lines, and of eight- and six-syllable lines, but they are not numerous.

The stanzas do not follow any determined pattern; their internal structure varies greatly. There are stanzas of twelve, ten, eight, six, and, above all, of four lines. Sometimes all the stanzas in a poem are identical, but the poet permits herself the liberty of altering them here and there. The strophic forms are not among the best-known kinds. The incomplete *seguidilla* is present only in some of the lullabies.

Except for two poems, "The Divine Memory" (*La memoria divina*) and "The Law of the Treasure" (*La ley del tesoro*), there are no perfect rhymes in the book. The rule is assonantal rhyme on the penultimate syllable of the even lines. There are, however, many instances of assonance on the last syllable. The same assonantal rhyme is kept throughout all the lines and only on a few occasions does it vary with the change of stanza.

From time to time the author takes a few deliberate liberties in order to break the monotonus and insistent succession:

In "The Flight" (*La fuga*), she omits the rhyme from one of the even lines toward the end of the poem.

In "Filial Gravestone" (*Lápida filial*), the rhyme is placed within the last line so that the end syllables are left without rhyme.

In "Bread" (*Pan*), there is an interruption of the rhyme in the last line of the stanza. The same technique is employed in "Drink" (*Beber*) and in "Mountain Range" (*Cordillera*).

The study of these technical details reveals the scanty attention that Gabriela Mistral paid to the mechanically formal aspect of her poetry. She preferred to direct her attention to the content of ideas and to the linguistic expression. Her rhythms are characterized by their regularity and their natural simplicity. The ballad form predominates—long stretches of eight-syllable lines with assonantal rhyme in the even lines, and the odd ones free. But the meter she most frequently employed was the nine-syllable line. This meter approaches the simplicity found in popular poetic forms, a musical ingenuity that is completely free of artifice. It has the parallelism of a prayer murmured in a low voice and the symmetric impact of a litany. It is the work not of a silversmith but of a sculptor.

Beside this, and in flagrant contrast, there are the broad, free, irregular unrhymed rhythms that so greatly resemble prose.

The poet was conscious of her tendency to prefer one meter and she tried to avoid it either by breaking the continuity of the rhyme at times or by introducing a dissonant note. The effect achieved in this manner produces surprise as well as jolting and slightly irritating the reader. The total impression on the ear of the reader is that of the slow, relentless flow of heavy water. Some lines are harsh; others, like those of the *seguidilla*, and especially the rhymes of the lullabies, possess the airy grace of folk poetry.

The Language   Gabriela frequently said that her aim was to make her written, poetic language come as close as possible to the oral forms of language. We believe that she realized this ideal in her prose; in her verse it was already at the point of flowering.

The linguistic expression in *Felling* avails itself of a rich vocabulary of common words in everyday use. Some of the expressions originate in the rural speech of Elqui and are endowed with the wit and vividness with which the people find names for objects and experiences. The abundance of diminutives and possessives give this lexicon affectionate overtones.

But side by side with this vernacular, there appear several *cultismos* (pure or learned linguistic forms), as well as numerous allusions to American geography, indigenous history, nature in all its forms, and the poet's readings. There is a predominance of terms with a religious sense and constant references to the Scriptures. The influence of the Bible on the poet's intellectual,

religious, and even literary formation is evident in all her work,
from *Desolation* on.

There is an originality of syntaxis in *Felling* that we had
formerly noted in Gabriela's prose. It is a difficult, somewhat
arbitrary syntaxis that seeks to capture fully both the idea and
the emotional connotations inherent in the mental image. Her
eagerness for psychological precision results in an involved,
closely-knit phrase that is often elliptical and obscure. She makes
constant use of reflexive forms. These forms, which would be
worth analyzing in detail, are evidence of Gabriela's warmth,
that manner of "walking hand in hand" or "heart to heart" with
the things of which she so often spoke.

The phrases follow a parallel or symmetrical structure. At
times they are carried along by the rhythm; at other times they
are determined by a pervading emotion of enthusiasm or religious ecstasy identical to that expressed in litanies or in biblical
verses. In some cases they are so dramatically forceful that they
seem to spring forth from the very heat of her blood.

The metaphors and images derive from the contemplation of
nature, from that telluric sense mentioned before, from her reli-
gious-Christian feeling; at times they are tinged with eroticism.
This recent poetry, in contrast to *Desolation*, speaks more of
ideas than feelings. Yet the attitude is very far from being an
intellectual one, for within the poet these ideas become passions,
"flesh of her flesh and blood of her blood." The poet views herself and her surroundings as one would a problem; but she lives
that problem with the force, sincerity, and ingenuity with which
emotions are lived. Her language is not tempered by logic nor
is it one of quiet abstractions. On the contrary, it moves spon-
taneously and in lightening flashes: it illuminates concepts but
does not develop them.

In general, the linguistic expression of *Felling* cuts and shapes
the ideas and feelings as the sculptor carves wood or stone. Both
real and ideal things acquire volume, weight, ample rhythm.
Instead of details, there are masses felt in all their gravity. Color
is lacking, as are the more subtle sensations. The tactile sense
gives us its exclusive definition of the world and its desires in
tangible, true forms. In one of the most interesting poems in the
group, the air itself takes on form and substance. From that

former hunger for dissolution into nothingness, which the poet expressed in the symbols of algae, shadow, and mist, she has now returned to the world of matter.

Aside from what this fact may mean in terms of the evolution of Gabriela's thought and poetry, it is important to note, at the same time, that the poet was also reflecting a general literary tendency of her time. Poets were returning to objectivity, to un-deniable reality free from the "I," a reality that had been lost to poetry ever since subjectivism reached its peak in the present century. Gabriela reflected this rediscovery in the section of *Felling* that she called "Matter" (*Materias*). But the material reality presented to us is enveloped in an ecstatic light. Familiar, daily experiences suddenly reveal to us their innermost, hidden secret; the poet discovers the visible presence of God in all things on this earth.

WINE PRESS (LAGAR)

Background Sixteen years after *Felling*, Gabriela published *Wine Press*,[7] her swan song. This book was also a selection that discarded much of what she had written during those years, as well as a mirror of the times in which the poet lived and of her personal life and suffering. They were sixteen terrible years for human society as a whole as well as for the individual. During this period were World War II, the Korean War, the Cold War; denouncing was promoted and rewarded, persecutions, concen-tration camps, refinements of physical and psychological tor-tures; forced, mass exodus, insecurity, suspicion, fear, hysteria, thermonuclear bombs. Those years saw such an absolute under-mining of values that peace became a "cursed word," [8] and those who wanted peace became suspect and persecuted; values were so monstrously perverted that the attempt to avoid war took the form of a senseless race for arms that became more and more lethal. These were the years, still not over, of loathing and "nausea."

These years were critical on the personal and psychological

7 *Lagar* (Santiago, Chile: Ediciones of the Pacific, 1954). *Tala* was published in 1938.
8 This is what Gabriela called it in a now famous article.

level as well. For Gabriela they brought continuous travel, the suicide of her friends, Stefan Zweig and his wife, and that of Juan Miguel Godoy, the nephew she had raised and loved as a son and who had died under obscure circumstances in the flower of his eighteenth year. They were also the years of her Nobel Prize for literature, the slow decline of her health, her premonition of imminent death. In those years, from 1938 to 1954, she constantly changed her place of residence. She returned to America on her way back from Europe. She visited Brazil, Uruguay, Argentina, Chile, and her native Elqui valley, Peru, Ecuador, Panamá, Cuba, Mexico, the United States. On two other occasions she again went to Europe and spent time in Nice and Naples. In 1945, in Stockholm, she received the highest literary recognition of all. Now she could permit herself the luxury of living wherever she chose: the Chilean government was always eager to honor her with a diplomatic post; Mexico made her a gift of some land; she purchased houses in Santa Barbara, California, and in Petropolis, Brazil. Every so often it would seem that she had finally found repose: she would light the fireplace, build a library, collect records of folk music and folk poetry, cultivate a garden and orchard, form a circle of friends. But she never stayed for long; once again she would move from one place to another, spurred on by something within herself, something that she had perhaps inherited from her roving, vagabond father. Over and over she renewed her wandering as one possessed, restless, as if fleeing, always reliving memories, dreaming of her little village of Montegrande, her Italian sea, tropical palm groves, the cornfields of her Mexico. The longest sojourns were in Nice, Brazil, Veracruz, and the United States. She left Nice because of the war and Brazil because she was shattered by the overwhelming triple suicide. Her last years were spent in the United States, first in New York, then in Washington, Miami, Monrovia, Santa Barbara, and finally, in Roslyn Harbor, Long Island. In spite of her now serious illness, she summoned strength to attend the Convention of writers on Martí in Cuba, the Lectures for Responsible Freedom at Columbia University, or to carry out her duties as a member of the Committee on Women's Rights of the United Nations.

All this left its trace in *Wine Press*. *Wine Press* is the inter-

nalization and poetic transfiguration of these events and experiences. The anecdotal element is as important here as in
the former books, although it is hidden behind a veil of hallucination and dream. The biographical reality is present, but always on the border of fantasy; always oscillating between the
real and the dreamed.

Title and Composition   The title of the work repeats that
image of the "Nocturne" (*Nocturno*) in *Desolation:*

> *¡Y en el ancho lagar de la muerte*
> *aun no quieres mi pecho exprimir!*

> And in the wide wine press of death
> You still will not drain my heart!

In the wine press of life and death, the poet has wrung from
herself the bitter juice of these lines, and she has been left ex-
hausted, as if emptied of herself. Now she no longer seeks death
with that passionate rebellion of youth and unrequited love. She
feels it "crossing the threshold"; she awaits it in silence, she wills
it. At times she seems to have crossed the line and no longer
knows whether she is dead or living; and she begins to converse
with her ghosts.

The book is made up of a Prologue, an Epilogue, and thirteen
sections. There is no prose included, nor are there any explana-
tory notes as there were in *Desolation*, *Tenderness*, and *Felling*.
All of this supposes a stricter evaluation of the lyrical product,
a greater security in her own creation, in the right to her own
language. Through "The Other One" (*La otra*), the poem that
serves as a prologue for Gabriela, we learn that she has left behind the ardor and sensuality of her young years;

Una en mí mate;	Let one in me be killed;
yo no la amaba.	I did not love her.
Era la flor llameando	She was the blazing flower
del cactus de montaña;	Of the mountain cactus;
era aridez y fuego;	She was barrenness and fire;
nunca se refrescaba.	She was never refreshed.
p. 9, lines 1–6.	

This poem now speaks to us of a different Gabriela, divested of
matter, spiritualized, reconciled to death. "The Other One" pre-

sides over the work and renews in verse the "Vow" (*Voto*) of
Desolation:

In these one hundred poems there lies bleeding a painful past, in
which my song was stained with blood in order to offer me some
respite. I leave it behind me like a dark ravine and up the more
clement sides I climb towards the spiritual plateaus, where a broad
light will finally fall on my days. From them I will sing words of
hope, without looking at my heart again: I will sing as a man of
mercy once wished to, to "console men." At thirty years of age,
when I wrote *The Decalogue of the Artist* [*El decálogo del artista*],
I stated this "Vow" [*Voto*].

p. 243.

The strange poem that serves as an epilogue, "Last Tree"
(*Ultimo árbol*), sings of the definitive dream in the fresh shade
of a tamarind or cedar tree, inheritor of

lo que tuve	What I had
de ceniza y firmamento,	Of ash and firmament
mi flanco lleno de hablas	What I had of voice
y mi flanco de silencio;	And what I had of silence;
Soledades que me dí,	Solitudes I gave myself
soledades que me dieron,	Solitudes given to me,
y el diezmo que pagué al rayo	And the tithe I paid to the
de mi Dios dulce y tremendo;	lightening bolt
	Of my sweet and tremendous
	God;
Mi juego de toma y daca	My game of give and take
con las nubes y los vientos,	With the clouds and winds,
y lo que supe, temblando,	And what I learned,
de manantiales secretos.	trembling,
p. 188, lines 21–32.	From secret springs.

Here she is surrendering her spiritual and moral self, not only
her body. She delineates her psychological traits in the firm
brush strokes of this exact self-portrait. Gabriela loved trees "as
one loves a man," a husband. Her treatment of them was that
of one person to another; it was an exaltation and personification that went beyond simple love for creatures or rustic familiarity with living things of the soil. The self-portrait reveals the
almost pantheistic face of the poet and her deification of nature.
In addition, trees and animals were the sources for numerous

affectionate names she gave people of whom she was fond, either in friendly conversation with them or in poetic treatment.

Una mujer

Cuando dice "pino de Alepo"
no dice árbol que dice un niño.
y cuando dice "regato"
y "espejo de oro," dice lo mismo.
                                    p. 87, lines 5–8.

A Woman

When she says "pine of Aleppo"
She does not mean a tree she means a child.
And when she says "rivulet"
And "golden mirror," she means the same.

"Cedar of Lebanon," "pine of Aleppo" is what she playfully or tenderly used to call her nephew, Juan Miguel. The frequency of "tree" [9] as an ideal term of comparison takes on symbolic purpose in these verses.

In the sections of *Wine Press*, we come across the repetition of titles from sections of *Desolation, Tenderness,* and *Felling;* [10] a reiteration that corresponds to the insistence and persistence of the following poetic motifs through all of her work:

[9] "Last tree" (*último árbol*), "tree of mourning" (*árbol de luto*), "my joy which is a tree" (*mi dicha que es un árbol*), "they free me from myself as from a tree" (*me descargan de mí misma como de árbol*), "tree, son" (*hijo árbol*).

[10] *Desolation* (*Desolación*): "Life" (*Vida*); "School" (*Escuela*); "For Children" (*Infantiles*); "Sorrow" (*Dolor*); "Nature" (*Naturaleza*).

Tenderness (*Ternura*): "Lullabies" (*Canciones de cuna*); "Rounds" (*Rondas*); "The Raving Woman" (*La desvariadora*); "Tricks" (*Jugarretas*); "The Story-World" (*Cuenta-mundo*); "Almost for School" (*Casi escolares*).

Felling (*Tala*): "Death of My Mother" (*Muerte de mi madre*); "Hallucination" (*Alucinación*); "Tales of a Madwoman" (*Historias de loca*); "Matter" (*Materias*); "America" (*América*); "Nostalgia" (*Saudade*); "The Dead Wave" (*La ola muerta*); "Creatures" (*Criaturas*); "Lullabies" (*Canciones de cuna*); "The Story-World" (*La cuenta-mundo*); "Messages" (*Recados*).

Wine Press (*Lagar*): "Fantasy" (*Desvarío*); "War" (*Guerra*); "Tricks" (*Jugarretas*); "Mourning" (*Luto*); "Madwomen" (*Locas mujéres*); "Nature" (*Naturaleza*); "Nocturnes" (*Nocturnos*); "Work" (*Oficios*); "Religious Verses" (*Religiosas*); "Rounds" (*Rondas*); "Wandering" (*Vagabundaje*); "Time" (*Tiempo*); "Earthly Message" (*Recado terrestre*).

Imaginative fantasies: "The Raving Woman" (*La desvaria-dora*); "Hallucination" (*Alucinación*); "Tales of a Madwoman" (*Historias de loca . . .*)

Evocations and nostalgia: "Nostalgia" (*Saudade*); "The Dead Wave" (*La ola muerta*); "Wandering" (*Vagabundaje*); "Joy" (*Albricias*)

Childhood and motherhood: "School" (*Escuela*); "For Children" (*Infantiles*); "Lullabies" (*Canciones de cuna*); "Rounds" (*Rondas*); "Tricks" (*Jugarretas*); "Almost for School" (*Casi escolares*); "Stories" (*Cuentos*)

Creatures, self-portraits: "Creatures" (*Criaturas*); "Madwomen" (Locas mujeres)

Love-pain-death: "Sorrow" (*Dolor*); "Death of My Mother" (Muerte de mi madre); "Mourning" (*Luto*); "Nocturnes" (*Nocturnos*)

Nature, living beings, and things: "Nature" (*Naturaleza*); "The Story-World" (*La cuenta-mundo*); "America"; "Time" (*Tiempo*); "Matter" (*Materias*); "Work" (*Oficios*); "Tricks" (*Jugarretas*)

Religion: "Religious verses" (*Religiosas*); poems dispersed through other sections

Circumstances: "Life" (*Vida*); "Messages" (*Recados*); "War" (*Guerra*); "Earthly Message" (*Recardo terrestre*)

The book lacks tonal unity. The poems within the group "Tricks" (*Jugarretas*), almost all those in the section "Nature" (*Naturaleza*), and the "Rounds" (*Rondas*) reveal to us the playful, mocking, happy Gabriela who lived side by side with the one of the tragic mask: a Gabriela of clear, capricious, and imaginative laughter, capable of running through the fields, embracing the trees, flinging herself to the ground to inhale, avidly, its fragrances; an elemental and bacchic creature, strongly attracted by a search for earthly happiness, entranced with the beauty of the world.

El reparto

Y otras tomen mis sentidos.
Con su sed y con su hambre,
p. 14, lines 23–24.

The Distribution

And let others take my senses.
With their thirst and with their hunger.

In "Eight Little Dogs" (*Ocho perritos*) this aspect of happiness is shown as the desire for instinctive life, though joined to the divine order of the creation:

Y yo querría nacer con ellos.	And I would want to be born
¿ Por qué otra vez no sería?	with them.
Saltar unos bananales	Why could it not be again?
una mañana de maravilla,	To jump through banana groves
en can, en coyota, en venada;	One miraculous morning,
mirar con grandes pupilas,	As a dog, coyote, or deer;
correr, parar, correr,	To gaze with large pupils,
tumbarme	To run and stop, run and fall
y gemir y saltar de alegría,	And whimper and jump for joy,
acribillada de sol y ladridos	Pierced by sun and barks
hija de Dios, sierva oscura	A daughter of God, humble and
y divina.	divine servant.

p. 36, lines 15–24.

The poetic motifs: religion The first section, "Fantasy" (*Desvarío*), contains only two poems: "The Distribution" (*El reparto*) and "Request for Blanca" (*Encargo a Blanca*), both on a religious theme—the divestment and distribution of the bodily senses after death, a return in spirit to communicate with the living. Some incidental confessions have psychological interests:

Encargo a Blanca

Y otras tomen mis sentidos . . .

Y no llores si no te respondo
porque mi culpa fué la palabra.
p. 15, lines 13–14.

Request for Blanca

And do not weep if I do not answer
For my sin was the word.

The religious beliefs are not clear, nor do they follow a definite body of dogma. Poetically at least, she seems to deny the resurrection of the flesh:

El reparto	The Distribution
Acabe así, consumada	Let me end thus, consummated
repartida como hogaza	Doled out like bread
y lanzada a sur o a norte	And flung to south or north
no seré nunca más una.	Never again to be one.
p. 14, lines 25–28.	

On the other hand, she alludes to the state of expiation of sins in the beyond (purgatory?):

> Y *no llores si no te respondo* ...

and to the communication between living and dead. She conceives of the beatific state as a pure vision, as all encompassing intelligence and knowledge:

El reparto	The Distribution
¿Ojos? ¿para qué preciso	Eyes? Why do I need them
arriba y llena de lumbres?	In the above, filled with lights?
En mi patria he de llevar	In my Country I am to wear
todo el cuerpo hecho pupila,	My whole body as an eye,
espejo devolvedor,	A reflecting mirror
ancha pupila sin párpados	A wide pupil without lids.
Iré yo a campo traviesa	I will run across the country
con los ojos en las manos	With my eyes in my hands
y las dos manos dichosas	And my two hands joyous,
deletreando lo no visto	Tracing the unseen
nombrando lo adivinado.	Naming what was guessed.
p. 13, lines 1–16.	

She calls paradise "my country" and the earth "my dwelling place." This stylistic trait was not found in former works. It consists of calling things by very personal, metaphorical names, written with a capital letter, at times modified by the first person possessive. It is as if, in this way, the poet were sentimentally and subjectively taking possession of things, attributing to them some extraordinary value and thus creating for herself her own universe.

It would be appropriate to add to this group the eight poems of the section "Religious Verses" (*Religiosas*). Three of them, "Indian Noël" (*Noël indio*), "Christmas Pines" (*Pinos de Navidad*), "Christmas Star" (*Estrella de Navidad*), objectively

deal with the theme of the Incarnation and belong to the class
of poems for children by virtue of their gay rhythm, graceful
images, and their form of story, ballad, and lullaby. "Indian Procession" (*Procesión india*) expresses ideas and images analogous
to the two hymns in *Felling*. The popular worship of Saint Rose
of Lima is evidence—as are the mountain range and the tropical
sun—of the eternal spiritual community of the American peoples. The blessing of food in "Lunch in the Sun" (*Almuerzo al
sol*) serves as a pretext for exalting the luminosity and plenitude
of noon. With almost mathematical conciseness, in the style of
Valéry, she evokes the table, the fruit, the gestures of the table
companions, setting them all into the harmonious rhythm, the
clean color, and the plastic imagery of a still life. The simple,
daily act is thus clothed in profound, ritualistic beauty.

Bendícenos la jarra	We are blessed by the jug
que abaja el cuello gresco,	That lowers its young neck,
la fruta embelesada,	The enchanting fruit,
la mazorca riendo,	The laughing corn,
y el café de ojo oscuro	And the dark-eyed coffee
que está empinado, viéndonos.	Tipped, and gazing at us.
Las grecas de los cuerpos	The graceful curves of
	bodies
bendígalas su Dueño;	Let the Lord bless them,
ahora el brazo en alto,	Now the arm on high
ahora el pecho,	Now the breast,
y la mano de siembras,	Now the hand that sows
y la mano de riegos.	And the hand that waters.
pp. 133–34, lines 17–28.	

"The Return" (*El regreso*) repeats the old philosophical common places of the dream of life, time's deception, the imperfec-
tion and vanity of human things, the great theatre of the world.
For the poet we are "unconscious, fanciful children" who, ex-
hausted by the game of life, return to the reality of the Eternal,
the only true land. "Memory of Grace" (*Memoria de la Gracia*)
returns to the theme of "Spotted Bird" (*Pajaro pinta*) in *Felling*,
even to the same rhythmic scheme. The poet tells of her experience with grace and delineates the religious experience—as did
the Spanish Mystics whom she frequently read—in a series of
admirable images that suggest lightness, rapidity, height, spirituality, light.

"War" (*Guerra*)   The section entitled "War" shows us a

Gabriela preoccupied with external events, no longer enclosed in the ivory tower. As in the case of the other Nobel laureate, Quasimodo, her verses capture the echoes of what is happening in the world, of the political and social problems of her time. World War II moves her to reflect upon the fate of Europe, to sing of the heroism of Finland, the lonely suffering of the wounded, the anguish of the persecuted and exiled. All the poems throb with the feeling of human solidarity in pain, with vehement protest against injustice, with the heroic sentiment of life; it is a moral conception of stoic strength modelled after Job and the Maccabees. Gabriela was incapable of considering political and social problems in the abstract. Being a woman, the essences moved her more than the historical situation. The human, private, personal case interested her above all. With her motherly tenderness and genuine charity, she would commit herself immediately, with great generosity and without reserve.

"The Trail" (*La huella*) is the best poem in this group. It is written in alternate lines of seven and five syllables, which are purposely grouped in three units: the flight, the identification with the pursued, and the discovery that the persecution extends to the ends of the earth and that it is impossible to stop it. The insistent rapidity of the rhythm, the continuous linking of enumerative series, and the precipitous, breathless rush of verbs communicate the impression of hasty flight, of anguish and relentless pursuit. The poet takes pity on the pursued, shields him, tries in vain to erase his tracks with the passionate gestures of a mother or lover:

¡Voy corriendo, corriendo	I come running, running,
la vieja Tierra,	Across the old Earth,
rompiendo con la mía	Shattering with my steps
su pobre huella!	Your poor trail!
¡O me paro y la borran mis	Else, I stop and my flying
locas trenzas,	locks erase it,
o de bruces mi boca	Or face down, my mouth
lame la huella!	Licks away your trail!

p. 24, lines 44–51.

The intensity of the feeling is revealed through the tenderness or force of some of the images:

Ni señales, ni nombre,	Neither signs, nor name,
ni el país, ni la aldea;	Nor the country nor the town;
solamente la concha	Only the moist shell of your
húmeda de su huella;	trail;
solamente esta sílaba	Only this syllable
que recogió la arena	Captured by the sand
¡y la Tierra-Verónica	And stammered to me
que me lo balbucea!	By the Veronica-Land!

. . . .

la huella, Dios mío,	The trail, my God, the
la pintada huella:	painted trail:
el grito sin boca,	The mouthless scream
la huella, la huella!	The trail, the trail!

. . . .

su marca de hombre	Its sign of a man
dulce y tremenda.	Tremendous and sweet.

             pp. 23–24, lines 5–12;
                 31–34; 41–42.

Two other poems, "The Prisoner's Woman" (*Mujer de prisionero*) and "Jewish Emigrant" (*Emigrada judía*), included under the headings "Madwomen" (*Locas mujeres*) and "Wandering" (*Vagabundaje*), are also inspired by contemporary conditions. The first poem deals with a theme that was of great concern to Gabriela because of its moral implications and its repercussions on the family life of prisoners. On her travels she would often visit prisons to speak with the inmates and comfort them, reminding them that their guardian angel was with them in their loneliness. As often as she could, she initiated steps—difficult and even risky at times—to have them released or to alleviate their suffering. She felt drawn to them by the bond of sorrow and the humble Christian awareness that we are all sinners. The second poem describes the spiritual state of the emigrants. If we remember that she spent her life wandering, far from her country or the lands she loved, we will understand why this portrait of the Jewish emigrants seems more like her own self portrait:

Tan sólo llevo mi aliento	So alone I carry my courage
y mi sangre y mi ansiedad.	And my anguish and my blood.
Una soy a mis espaldas	One of me always looking
otra volteada al mar:	behind

mi nuca hierve de adioses,
y mi pecho de ansiedad.
. . . .
¡y aventada mi memoria
llegaré desnuda al mar!
    pp. 170–171; lines 13–18;
    29–30.
	The other thrust into the
	  sea:
	My neck wracked by farewells
	And my breast by fear.
	. . . .
	And with my billowing memory
	I will come naked into the
	  sea!

One would also place within the poems that reflect contemporary conditions the "Earthly Message" (*Recado terrestre*), an invocation to a sanctified Goethe to return to the world its lost vitality, to imbue the world with "his river of life."

"Poems for Children" (*Infantiles*) In the sections entitled "Tricks" (*Jugarretas*), "Rounds" (*Rondas*), and "Nature" (*Naturaleza*), there are lullabies, eulogies, and descriptions of things and landscapes. Some poems resemble others already published in former books: thus, "Helpers" (*Ayudadores*) (pp. 29–30), which voices maternal pride in the son who has grown into manhood, is reminiscent of "Requests" (*Encargos*) in *Felling* (pp. 204–206); "The Little Box of Raisins" (*Cajita de pasas*) (pp. 30–31), with its tender nostalgia for her native valley, recalls the "Little Box of Olinalá" (*La cajita de Olinalá*) in *Tenderness* (pp. 101–103).

The delicious description of the "Birth of a House" (*Nacimiento de una casa*) sings of the happiness of work, of little tasks like playful gnomes, of the sense of mystery and religiosity that the poet attributes to everything, even to material things. This ability to enhance the everyday, the commonplace, and the ordinary, how much it reminds us of the magic genius of Lope! Gabriela's reading of some of the Spanish classical writers has left profound imprints on her style.

Almost all of the "Rounds" (*Rondas*), in spite of their marked rhythmic pattern so similar to children's chants, are very adult, subjective descriptions—of the Argentinian land, varied fragrances, the royal palms, the fires on the night of San Juan. One notes in them the animation of motionless things, the personification of animals and plants so common in this poetry: a bacchic vision surrendering itself to the frenzied joy of the dance, to the sensuality of pure movement. "Round of Fragrances" (*Ronda de los aromas*) could inspire a Walt Disney fantasy or a festive ballad by Quevedo; in the "Cuban Round" (*Ronda cubana*), there is a repetition of the same spiritualization of the Puerto Rican palm grove as in "Caribbean Sea" (*Mar Caribe*); and what careful elaboration, what grace of rhythm and word, what folkloric charm in the "Round of the Fire" (*Ronda del fuego*), a very beautiful stylization of popular dance, a happy fusion of intellectuality and instinct, in which one hears echoes of Spanish classical writers, melodies of the popularist Lope and Góngora.

"Nature" (*Naturaleza*) In addition to the theme of the natural beauty of the Americas as a source of inspiration, we find in *Wine Press* the description of the palm groves of Cuba, the desert of Arizona, a Brazilian orchard, not formerly sung to, and the new themes of the poppy, the okote pine, the dry silkcotton tree, the Uruguayan corn tassel, the stone of Parahibuna, the pruning of trees, the rose bush and the almond tree. Here nature continues to be an inexhaustible mine of allusions, comparisons, images and, at times, a projection of the inner spiritual being. Her way of looking at it is very far from the romantic subjectivism and the mental landscapes of *Desolation*. In these poems, a profound, contemplative vision of strong religious roots predominates. They seem to soothe the spirit of the contemporary reader. In our century of urbanism, over indus trialization, and technology, of productivity without creativity, in a world that is increasingly anti-natural and unreal, the necessity for contact with nature is becoming a question of life or death. Man must return to his center, to live in a more natural and simple fashion, to re-incorporate himself into the rhythm of the cosmos, if he is to preserve the integrity of his person, his whole and true humanity. These verses console because they are the reflection of a human spirit that had always maintained an ardent relationship with the real and fundamental things in life: with God, the earth, sex, love, death; of a spirit uncontaminated by the destructive viruses of our materialistic, artificial, and skeptical civilization. The poet's childhood was spent in the country, among mountains, in direct, joyful, imaginative, free communication with plants and animals, with clouds and stars; her child's hands helped in the agricultural chores, in the kind of manual workmanship that

does not breed dulling routine nor blunt the creative faculties.
Her poems on nature are descriptions, eulogies of living things:
behind the veil of their bright sensorial beauty, they reveal their
true essence, their mystery. The poet personifies and spiritualizes
these living beings; she gazes at them with warmth and reverence. She sees them not as isolated objects, not as food for
sensual pleasure, but as living parts of an organism, phases of
the harmony that sings the perennial psalm of praise to the
Creator. She can say of the California poppy:

En la palma apenas duras	In my palm you hardly last
y recoges, de tomada,	And plucked, you withdraw
como unos labios sorbidos	Your four words rapidly
tus cuatro palabras rápidas,	Like tasted lips,
cuando te rompen lo erguido	When they break your lofty
y denso de la alabanza.	Full-bodied beauty.
p. 93, lines 13–18.	

Her approach to these things is that of the child: rapt, imaginative, mythological:

Canción del maizal	Song of the Cornfield
Las mazorcas del maíz	The ears of corn
a niñitas se parecen:	Look like little girls:
diez semanas en los tallos	Ten weeks in the stalks
bien prendidas que se mecen.	Tightly held they sway.
Tiene un vellito de oro	They have little golden fuzz
como de recién nacido	Like that of new-born babes
y unas hojas maternales	And motherly leaves
que les celan el rocío.	Shield them from the dew.
Y debajo de la vaina	And within the sheath
como niños escondidos,	Like little children hidden,
con sus dos mil dientes de	With two thousand golden
oro	teeth
ríen, ríen sin sentido.	They laugh and laugh without
p. 108, lines 17–28.	reason.

Or her approach is that of the mother: tender, protective, sym-
pathetic:

Ceiba seca	Dry Silkcotton Tree
Llano y cielo no me ayudan	Neither plain nor heaven help
a acostarla en rojas gredas	me
con el rocío en su espalda	To lay her to rest on red clay

y el Zodíaco en sus guedejas.	With the dew on her back
antes que las hachas lleguen,	And the Zodiac in her locks.
mascullando un santo salmo,	Before the axes come,
tengo que entregarla al fuego.	Mumbling a holy psalm,
p. 110, lines 21–24; 26–28.	I must offer her to the fire.

And always there is the attitude of the true poet who recreates and beautifies, who knows how to see beyond appearances, who listens in the silence and senses the true significance:

La piedra de Parahibuna	The Stone of Parahibuna
Parece mi Cordillera	My mountain range seems
abajada, sierva y junta.	Lower, humble and close.
Parece Madre-Elefanta,	She looks like Mother
y el regazo que más dura	Elephant,
y la voz que más aúpa.	The lap that is always
Parece el haz de una Gloria,	waiting
y el perdón de nuestras	And the voice the child still
culpas,	heeds.
y de lo ancha que es, la	It is like the face of Glory,
noche,	And the pardon for our sins,
a ella no más arrebuja.	So broad she is, she can no
	longer
	Be wrapped in the night.
Buena para hacer la ofrenda	Good to make an offering
y alzar a lo alto su aleluya,	And raise on high her praise,
para encender una hoguera	To light a fire
u ofrecer desnudo un hijo	Or offer naked, her son
o morir dando el espíritu	Or die, with the spirit
de muerte aceptada y pura.	Of death accepted and pure.
pp. 97–98, lines 7–21.	

Gabriela captures both the earthly and cosmic sense of these beings; they appear to her as steps that link her to God and to the earth, as understandable words and signs of the earthly and the Eternal. At times this objective vision, so realistic and penetrating it impels the poet to communion with the universe, gives way, through some image or analogy, to a subjective, personal reference. Then the buried vein breaks through the words and sheds its brief drop of bitterness on the song of praise:

Ocotillo	Little Okote Pine
Cuando para y cae rota	When the storm stops
la borrasca, y no hay senderos,	Broken, and there are no
voy andando, voy llegando	paths,

a su magullado cuerpo
y lo oscuro y lo ofendido
yo le enjugo y enderezo
—como aquél que me
*   troncharon—*
con la esponja de mi cuerpo,
y mi palma lo repasa
en sus miembros que son
*   fuego.*
    p. 104, lines 37–46.

I keep walking, closer to
Its mangled body
And what is dark and violated
I dry and straighten
—So like the one they cut
    from me—
With the sponge of my body,
And my palm runs over
Its fiery limbs.

But the references are incidental; the poet has gained in wisdom, in forgetfulness of self.

Let us point out as a singular, perhaps unique, element in Gabriela's work the beautiful description of the Arizona desert as pure negation and emptiness; this stands in marked contrast to the ardent affirmation of the okote pine:

Ocotillo

Little Okote Pine

Rasa patria, raso polvo,
raso plexo del desierto;
duna y dunas enhebradas,
y hasta Dios, rasos los
*   cielos,*
todo arena voladora
y sólo él permaneciendo;
toda hierba consumada
y no más su grito entero.

Flat country, flat dust,
Flat plexus of the desert;
Threads of dune and dunes,
And even God, flat the
    heavens,
All is flying sand
It alone endures;
All the green consumed
Its scream alone is whole.

Dice "¡no!" la vieja arena
y el blanquear del cantor
*   muerto,*
y el anillo de horizonte
dice "¡no!" a su prisionero,
y Diós dice "¡sí!" tan sólo
por el ocotillo ardiendo.
    pp. 103–104, lines 15–28.

The ancient sand says "No!"
And the whitened song bird's
    bones
And horizon's ring
Says "No!" to its prisoner,
And God, through the burning
    pine alone
Says "Yes!"

There is also the curious poem, "Death of the Sea" (*Muerte del mar*), the only one in this group that is negative in mood, a fantasy similar to the one in "Child-Death" (*Muerte-Niña*) of *Felling*. As in the darkest surrealistic nightmare, the sea basin is drained and reveals to the terrified eyes of the fishermen a livid, oppressive, chilling landscape.

Quedaron las madreperlas
y las caracolas lívidas
y las medusas vaciadas
de su amor y de sí mismas.

Quedaban dunas-fantasmas
más viudas que la ceniza,
mirando fijas la cuenca
de su cuerpo de alegrías.

Y la niebla, manoseando
plumazones consumidas,
y tanteando albatros muerto,
rondaba como la Antígona.
　　　p. 100, lines 29–40.

Only the mother of pearls
　　remained
And livid snails
And jellyfish emptied
Of their love and of
　　themselves.

Only phantom dunes remained
More widowed than the ash,
Gazing fixed at the basin
Of their body's joys.

And the mist, rippling
Wasted feathers,
Prodding a dead Albatross,
Circled like Antigone.

The life-death contrast, so often repeated in Gabriela's work, can be clearly seen when we compare these poems with the other poems in "Nature" (*Naturaleza*), ardent hymns of movement and joy. The vision of the desert, the death of the sea reveal to us the poet's instinctive and intuitive rejection of everything anti-natural, disordered, dead. In nature she loved the movement, the power of the elements, the vital forces of germination, growth, transformation, and change. Her adherence to the Christian conception of death as the seed and promise of a fuller, more real life is the logical consequence of these premises.

An incidental landscape, inserted into the "Fall of Europe" (*Caída de Europa*), reminds us of the beautiful evocations in the "General Song" (*Canto general*) by the Chilean poet Pablo Neruda:

> *Solamente la Gea americana*
> *vive su noche con olor de trébol,*
> *tomillo y mejorana y escuchando*
> *el rumor de castores y de martas*
> *y la carrera azul de la chinchilla.*
> 　　　p. 19, lines 13–17.

> Only the American Earth Spirit
> Lives its night with the fragrance of clover,
> Thyme and sweet marjoram and listening
> To the sounds of beaver and marten
> And the blue-streaked flight of chinchillas.

Although the point of view and poetic treatment of the four poems dedicated to time (under the heading "Time" (*Tiempo*) are so different, we might perhaps consider them as part of the group "Nature" (*Naturaleza*). In them the poet sings of her intimate experience with Chronos. The passing of the hours keeps changing her mental state, tingeing it with emotions that reflect the change of time: the fullness that expands the heart, in "Dawn" (*Amanecer*); the happiness of renewed hope, in "Morning" (*Mañana*); the "heavy oil" of sweetness, in "Dusk" (*Atardecer*); oblivion and the plunge toward death, in "Night" (*Noche*). The language and music of the verses flow serenely and clearly in their brevity. Each poem is developed rapidly, as a deliberate allusion to the fugacity of time. The most beautiful one of all, by virtue of its compactness, its profound simplicity, and the intimate richness it reveals is reminiscent of some of Antonio Machado's poetry or the *kasida* of some Arabic-Andalusian poet.

Atardecer

Siento mi corazón en la dulzura
fundirse como ceras:
son un óleo tardo
y no un vino en mis venas,
y siento que mi vida se va huyendo
callada y dulce como la gacela.

p. 179.

Dusk

I feel my heart melt into
The sweetness like wax:
It is a heavy oil
And not a wine in my veins,
And I feel life fleeing
Silent and sweet as the gazelle.

But this poetic mode remains marginal to the general tone of *Wine Press*.

"Crafts" (*Oficios*) The interesting "Sonnets of Pruning" (*Sonetos de la Poda*), the poems in the section "Crafts" (*Oficios*) and the already referred to "Birth of a House" (*Nacimiento de una casa*), from the section "Tricks" (*Jugarretas*), express the love and respect that Gabriela felt for manual work and her affectionate interest in workers. She greatly admired the dexterity of the craftsman, and she knew that a work made directly by the hand of man is a creation of his spirit, stamped with the imprint of his inner life. She knew the pleasure, the love, and the pride with which the true artisan takes great pains to do his work well, to put into it the best of himself. (How different from the worker desensitized by industrial routine, corrupted by class hatred and the hunger for wealth, or made bitter by economic injustices!) Like the artist, the artisan creates beauty, shuns repetition, instinctively rejects the asceptic, almost repellent, ugliness of machine-made products.

For Gabriela work was a happy and creative activity that also had locked within it its mystery, its relationship to God and to the earth. She regarded tools with brotherly tenderness because they complement the hand of man, they help and accompany him in his labor and directly or indirectly they play a part in the decisive moments of his life. In the poem entitled "Tools" (*Herramientas*), she describes and humanizes them; she speaks and laughs with them; she makes requests of them; she attributes gestures of passion or of feminine tenderness to them:

Herramientas

Revueltas con los aperos,
trabados los pies de hierbas
trascienden a naranjo herido
o al respiro de la menta.
Cuando mozas brillan de ardores
y rotas son madres muertas.

. . . .

Toque a toque la azada viva
me mira y recorre entera
y le digo que me dé
al caer la última tierra;
y con ternura de hermana
yo la suelto, ella me deja . . .

pp. 127–128,
lines 13–18, 41–48.

Tools

Heaped among the farm tools,
The stalks of cuttings tied
They smell of wounded orange tree
Or of the breath of mint.
When maidens glow with ardor

And shattered are dead mothers.

. . . .
Stroke by stroke the living hoe
Looks at me and vigorously toils
And I beg it to give me
The last bit of earth as it falls;
And with a sister's tenderness
I release her, she leaves me . . .

The praise of the "Worker's Hands" (*Manos de obreros*)
evokes their "tremendous beauty," their silent understanding
with the earth. They are the hands of farmers, fishermen,
miners, weavers, marked with the painful imprints of time,
work, and material; anonymous hands that toil for us, as wise
in the weaving of children's clothing as in digging the grave:

> *y mi huesa la harán justa*
> *aunque no vieron mi espalda.*
> p. 130, lines 27–28.

And they will fit my tomb to me
Though they have not seen my measure.

Christ takes pity on them and when they rest from their labors

> *las toma y retiene*
> *entre las suyas hasta el Alba.*
> p. 130, lines 41–42.

He takes them and holds them
Between his own until Dawn.

In verses of classical pattern, with soberly restrained baroque
words and images, the poet describes the pruning of a rose bush,
an almond tree, and a tree in wintry slumber. The pruning is
carried out not only with knowledge and ability but also with
the participation of the spiritual powers and the emotions. It
is an action that is both intellectual and moral; a true creation,
like that of a poem or the education of a son. Of all the poems
in *Wine Press*, these are the most elaborately styled, the most
cerebral and elegant. But they are also the least Mistralian in
tone and form.

Beneath the heading "Wandering" (*Vagabundaje*), there
appear "Jewish Emigrant" (*Emigrada judía*), already com-
mented upon, "Good-by" (*Adiós*), and "Countries" (*Patrias*),

songs of farewell to the Elqui valley, "the land of two years, golden as Epiphany," to Provence, "of light-oiled happiness," to Liguria, "matron and damsel," and to Mexico with its "jades that soon will speak"; lands she loved very much, faithful as mothers, always ready to welcome home the prodigal son and whose beauty she describes with the warm tenderness of nostalgia.

Patrias

No son mirajes de arenas;
son madres en soledad.
Dieron el flanco y la leche
y se oyeron renegar.
Pero por si regresásemos
nos dejaron en señal
los pies blancos de la ceiba
y el rescoldo del faisán.

p. 173, lines 27–34.

Countries

They are not sand mirages;
They are mothers in loneliness.
They gave their bodies and milk
And heard themselves disowned.
But should we wish to return
They have left us as a sign
The white trunk of the silk cotton tree
And the pheasant's ember glow.

"Leave-taking" (*Despedida*) is a farewell to the world with "the throat slashed." Yet at the same time, it is an offer of thanksgiving for all of the world's material blessings: bread, salt, the bed "fragrant with mint." The poet prepares herself to end her wandering in time and to join the "living shoal of its dead." The "Doors" (*Puertas*) are the symbol of all limitations. They prevent communication with nature; closed, they let destiny pass.

Puertas

Y lo mismo que Casandra,
no salvan aunque sepan;
porque mi duro destino
el también pasó mi puerta.

p. 166, lines 33–36.

Doors

And the same as Cassandra,
They may know, yet do not save;
Because my cruel destiny
Has also passed my door.

The poet personifies the doors as she does all other material objects—"never young girls, always old," or she animalizes them —"sad mollusks without tide or sand," and she clothes them in mystery. As she crosses their thresholds for the last time, she will achieve the complete liberty of death.

Sorrow, death "Mourning" (*Luto*), "Madwomen" (*Locas mujeres*), and "Nocturnes" (*Nocturnos*) form a closely knit unit revolving around the single theme of sorrow at the death of Juan Miguel, her nephew. Loved by Gabriela with motherly tenderness, Juan Miguel grew up in her shadow from the time he was a child; he was her companion, the strongest bond that tied her to life. Beside him she walked through the world; for him she stopped to light the hearth; for him she worked and provided. She had taken her leave of Eros and into this purer relationship she poured all the intensity of her passion, her "thirst and hunger," the longings of frustrated motherhood. In him she saw the bough that would soon flower, bringing her compensation for not having a "son, or mother, or living clan"; and, as she says in "Fall of Europe" (*Caída de Europa*), for the bitterness of "prayers that echoed against the empty air and walls" (p. 19, lines 3–5). But just as the moment of the boy's spiritual maturity was approaching, and with it the possibility of a fuller love and more perfect communion between them, Juan Miguel committed suicide one nightmarish night, for reasons that have not been completely clarified to this day. Gabriela spent that night at the dying boy's bedside, alone, mute, face to face with the terrible experience of death.

Luto	Mourning
En lo que dura una noche	In the space of a night
cayó mi sol, se fué mi día,	My sun fell, my day fled,
y mi carne se hizo humareda	And my flesh became smoke
que corta un niño con la mano.	Cut by the hand of a child.
p. 46, lines 35–38.	

"The Naked Side" (*El costado desnudo*) translates into verses of tragic beauty the anguish of this wound, like that of Christ's, the sensation of a mutilated body and soul:

Otra vez sobre la Tierra	Once before over the Earth
llevó desnudo el costado,	He bore his naked side

el pobre palmo de carne,	The poor handful of flesh
donde el morir es más rápido	Where dying is faster
y la sangre está asomada	And the blood is seeping
como a los bordes del vaso.	through
	As over the brim of a glass.
Va el costado como un vidrio	The side moves like glass
de sien a pies alargado	Stretched from temple to feet
o en el despojo sin voz	Or like the cluster harvested
del racimo vendimiado,	In a voiceless plunder,
y más desnudo que nunca,	And more naked than ever,
igual que lo desollado.	As one who has been flayed.

p. 41, lines 1–12.

Miguel's absence, his dark passing, became an obsession with her, paralyzing her will to live. She awaited death now without fear, willing it. At times it seemed to her that she had already experienced it and was enjoying beforehand the taste of the Eternal.

Aniverario / Anniversary

Y seguimos, y seguimos,	And we go on and on,
ni dormidos ni despiertos,	Neither sleeping nor awake,
hacia la cita e ignorando	Towards the meeting, unaware
que ya somos arribados.	That we are already there.
Y del silencio perfecto,	That the silence is perfect,
y de que la carne falta,	And that the flesh is gone.
la llamada aún no se oye	The call still is not heard
ni el Llamador da su rostro.	Nor does the Caller reveal his face.
. . . .	. . . .
¡Pero tal vez esto sea	But perhaps this might be
¡ay! amor mío, la dádiva	Oh, my love, the gift
del Rostro eterno y sin gestos	Of the eternal Face without gestures
y del reino sin contorno!	And of the kingdom without form!

p. 40, lines 45–56.

The senses and energies of her entire being break free from the world of earthly things and living beings; she projects upon them the sensation of absolute emptiness and exile that dominates her:

Mesa offendida

Nunca me he sentado a mesa
de mayor despojamiento:

la fruta es sin luz, los vasos
llegan a las manos hueros.
Tiene el pan de oro vergüenza
y el mamey un agrio ceño;
en torpe desmaño cumplen
loza, mantel, vino muerto,
y los muros dan la espalda
para no tocar el protervo.
Y ellos del alma reciben
la respuesta de heno seco
y su mirada perdida
de pura ausencia y destierro.

pp. 47–48, lines 21–34.

Offended Table

Never have I sat down to a table
Of greater barrenness:
The fruit is without light, the glasses
Come to my hands, empty.
The golden bread is ashamed
And the mamey wears a bitter frown;
Together in dull disarray
Plates, cloth, dead wine,
And the walls turn their backs
To avoid the wantonness.
And they receive from the soul
The answer of dried hay
And its lost look
Of pure absence and exile.

She lives with her face to the beyond, in silent and constant dialogue with her dead: with her mother to whom she calls in her loneliness, with Juan Miguel whose presence fills her hallucinations and nightly fantasies, to whom she speaks with words and names of heart-rending tenderness:

Canto que amabas

Yo canto lo que tú amabas, vida mía
por si te acercas y escuchas, vida mía,
por si te acuerdas del mundo que viviste,
al atardecer yo canto, sombra mía.

Yo no quiero enmudecer, vida mía,
¿Cómo sin mi grito fiel me hallarías?
¿Cuál señal, cuál me declara, vida mía?

.   .   .   .

Te espero sin plazo y sin tiempo.
No temas noche, neblina ni aguacero.
Ven igual con sendero o sin sendero.
Llámame adónde eres, alma mía,
Y marcha recto hacia mí, compañero.
p. 23, lines 1–7; 14–18.

The Song You Loved

I sing of what you once loved, life of mine,
Should you approach and listen, life of mine,
Should you recall the world you lived in,
At dusk I sing, shadow of mine.

I will not be silent, life of mine,
How will you find me without my faithful cry?
What sign will lead you to me, life of mine?

I await you without limit, without time.
Do not fear night, nor mist, nor rain.
Come, whether there be path or not.
Call to tell me where you are, oh soul of mine,
And walk straight toward me, dearest friend.

At times, there is almost an excessive idealization of the absent one in these verses: it is almost deification. The phantom presence of Juan Miguel plunges her into moments of agony that exhaust her; it impels her to break the barriers, to do violence to fate.

La desvelado

Los peldaños de sordo leño
como cristales me resuenan.
Yo sé en cuáles se descansa
y se interroga, y se contesta.
Oigo dónde los leños fieles,
igual que mi alma, se le quejan,
y sé el paso maduro y último
que iba a llegar y nunca llega . . .
p. 66, lines 29–36.

Sleepless Vigil

The steps of dull wood
Echo like tinkling glass.
I know on which he rests
Questioning himself, and answering.

I hear the faithful wood
Like my soul lament to him,
And I know the full, final step
That was coming and never came.

Or she attains a kind of mystical communion with the beloved,
who has become the only reason for life and hope. This plenitude is like an anticipation of the vision of God.

Los dos

Miguel y yo nos miramos
como era antes, cuando la tierra,
cuando la carne, cuando el Tiempo
y la noche sin sus estrellas.
                    p. 49, lines 17–20.

We Two

Miguel and I gaze at each other
As it was then, at the time of earth,
At the time of flesh, and that of Time
And the night without its stars.

Todavía somos el Tiempo,
pero probamos ya el sorbo
primero, y damos el paso
adelantado y medroso.
Y una luz llega anticipada
de la Mayor que da la mano,
y convida, y toma, y lleva.

We are still Time
Yet already we take the first taste
And we step
forward and fearful.
And there comes a light, awaited
From the Eldest who gives her hand
And beckons, and takes, and carries.

The series of beautiful poems called "Madwomen" (Locas
mujeres) described with detailed clarity the various moods, the
facets that pain has etched into the soul of this Antigone so
passionately obsessed with the funeral rite. This section is an
unfolding and personification of her emotions, self-portraits that
nakedly reveal her "passion," the terrifying emptiness about her,

and the self-willed anticipation of death as a longed for liberation. The reader looks out on these abysses where gesticulating
creatures writhe—the abandoned, the anxious, the dancers, the
forsaken, the watchful, the fervent, the pious, those who wander,
the humiliated—like figures in a medieval morality. And one is
astonished at the implacable self-analysis, the dark pleasure—
so modern—in the convolutions of the "I." It is a revelation, in
poetic symbols, of the silent battle with the angel, of the terrible
stamp of God on the thigh:

> *el diezmo que pagué al rayo*
> *de mi Dios dulce y tremendo.*

> The tithe I payed to the lightening bolt
> Of my sweet and tremendous God.

Language and style   When compared to the former books,
Wine Press reveals its own individualities of language and style.
It represents the results of an evolution that has progressively
purified the lyricism of romantic overtones, infusing it with
greater objectivity and simplicity. The effort to fit the language
more closely to the poetic intent is more evident here than in the
past. The poet has not lost any of her intuitive spontaneity,
imaginative force, or intensity; however, she develops those
materials with greater deliberation and care. In this way she
evolves a language free of encumbrances, relieved of sensuality
and sentimentalism. Her voice has the dry, crackling ardor of
the Psalmists and the Prophets, without any pleasure in the
sensory values of the word. The almost complete absence of
color, of sonorous and melodic effects, and of descriptions of
shape and movement is not capricious: the lineal elements
supersede the musical and pictorial ones. The result is an
asceticism that imparts severity and vigor to the language.

While the vocabulary retains archaic forms, peculiarly American expressions, and idioms of popular, regional origin, they are
already fewer in number when compared to the lexicon of her
prose writings and of her earlier poetry.

On the other hand, one notes an unusual abundance of references, of learned forms and Latinisms, some phonetic, some
semantic. The most insistent references pertain, naturally, to
American geography, to its fauna and, above all, to its flora.

There are also astronomical, mythological, biblical, religious, and literary references.[11] The direct observation of reality, rural childhood, the cosmic emotion, religious probing, the reading of the Bible and of the Graeco-Roman classics provide these allusions. Within the group of Latinisms and cultismos, scarce in her former work, there seems to exist a decided preference for words of antepenultimate stress (*alácrita, acérrimo, frenético, pávido, vívido*). This may perhaps be determined by the metric needs of the verse line or by the desire to produce certain sonorous effects. This kind of excessive correctness is heightened by a notable reduction in the number of regional and vernacular expressions. The *cultismos* are found especially in such poems as "Finnish Champion" (*Campeón Finlandés*), "Fall of Europe" (*Caída de Europa*), "Sonnets of Pruning" (*Sonetos de la poda*), "Earthly Message" (*Recado terrestre*). Because of the serious tone of these poems and the need to suit the lexicon to the theme and to the elegant metric form, the *cultismos* are quite appropriate.

The poet retains her preference for strong words of violent, unabashed realism—ardor, fervor, fire, to rend, wound, open, break, slice, scorch, flay, singe—because the tendency to emphasize remains a characteristic trait of her language.

We have already alluded to the novelty of creating names of her own through the conversion of adjectives; in this way she emphasizes the distinctive quality of the person in question, the

---

11 *Geographical*—Anahuac, Montegrande, Argentina, Arizona, California, Guayas, Mayab, Siboney, Parahibuna.

Fauna—albatross, alpaca, ostrich, ermine, beaver, bison, gull, civet cat, chinchilla, vicuña, gazelle.

Flora—carob tree, birch, almond tree, poppy, cactus, mahogany, silk-cotton, giant cedar, hawthorn, lignum-vitae, mamey, okote pine, mango, palm, pitahaya, pine, banana tree.

Astronomy—Bull's Eye, Andromeda, Libra, Sirius, Orion, Taurus, the Milky Way, zodiac.

Mythology—Demetrius, Erine, the Earth Spirit, Gorgon, Hades, Hebe, Minerva, Cybille, Dedalus.

Biblical—Abraham, Cain, David, Cirineus, Holofernes, Ismael, Job, Maccabees, Martha, Peter, Tobias, Veronica, the Olive Grove, Jordan.

Religious—angel, dominations, choirs, grace, Noël, Santa Rosa of Lima, Saint Dominick.

Literary—Antigone, Cassandra, Cordelia, Roland, Erasmus, Goethe, Félibres.

quality that has the greatest significance and expressive value for the poet: watchman, deaf one, raving one, mad one, caller, the eldest.

The peculiarities of syntax create a still more personal style. They are of even greater interest than the vocabulary, not so much for their novelty as for the author's technique of cumulative repetition. The outstanding characteristics of the syntax are a tendency toward multiple-clause sentences, enumerations in series of phrases of parallel structure, and repetitions of words, phrases, and lines. In this way the poet achieves effects of rapidity, emphasis, monotony, or intensity. The reader feels himself pulled along by a succession of things, allusions, images, as if he were obliged to follow the curve of a parabola.

The marked affectionate quality of the poetic language is heightened by the use of diminutives, possessives, datives, exclamatory sentences, interjections, rhetorical questions, and forms of address of the most intimate tenderness. There is a predominance of simply constructed affirmative sentences, of relative phrases that describe acts rather than qualities. All of this, in addition to the extraordinary wealth of verbs, imparts movement to the language; but frequently it is also responsible for its falling into the flowing, slack rhythm of prose.

There is a lack of fullness and melodic variety in the phrase. Its intonational curve is only slightly modulated and shaded, as in that of a prayer or confidence. There is created a general impression of monotony, of muted tones. One must exclude from this generalization the sections "Tricks" (*Jugarretas*) and "Rounds" (*Rondas*), where the imitation of folkloric melodies create charmingly light, vivacious, graceful effects.

The metric rhythm lacks variety. Most of the poems follow the pattern of the eight- or nine-syllable ballad, with the exception of the "Sonnets of Pruning" (*Sonetos de la poda*), the incomplete *seguidillas*, the couplets in which some of the "Rounds" (*Rondas*) and "Tricks" (*Jugarretas*) are written, the free hendecasyllable line in the solemn, heroic poems, and some anasyllabic combinations that put into play lines of five, six, seven, eight, nine, ten, eleven, twelve, and fourteen syllables. There are also little ballads of six- and seven-syllable lines. The free eleven-syllable lines and the anasyllabic combinations con-

vey fullness and rhythmic majesty; the varieties of the ballad
form create an impression of singsong; the *seguidillas* and
couplets embody the agile movement of dance.

There is a certain uncertainty in the measure of the initial
lines. At the beginning of the poem the poet seems to be seeking a rhythm without seeming to find it; after the fourth or
fifth line, the testing stops and the rhythm flows surely, without
vacillation. There is, likewise, a lack of complete control of the
rhyme; there are combinations of perfectly rhymed assonants,
changes of rhyme within the poem itself; the adopted model is
not faithfully followed. The assonances or consonances are imperfect and they deviate from the established rules.[12] Again, as
in the preceding works, unaccented words (*si, que, sobre, tan*)
occupy a position of rhyme or stand at the end of the line.

The poet is not concerned with melodic or rhythmic beauty;
she does not attempt to produce pleasant or harmonious auditory effects. She tends to monorhyme, to a music of dissonantal
harmonies. She does not have a good ear; her musical sensitivity
is neither elegant nor refined. The line that is most natural to
her suggests the sounds of nature, the low-voiced singing that
accompanies absorption in work, the whispers and prayers of
women, the murmur of someone who speaks to himself, not
wishing to be heard. This music, however, is very well suited
to the poetic themes because it intensifies the mournful, funereal
tone of most of the poems.

The manipulation of the adjective, as a stylistic technique, is
of extreme importance in *Wine Press*. We should consider it
more from the standpoint of the role of imagination in this work
than as a mere element of the lexicon. There is an overabundance of adjectives. They are even grouped in twos and
threes. There is hardly a noun that does not carry with it its
real or figurative modifier. The poet is not as interested in
specifying the palpable qualities of things—color, form, sound,
taste, smell, texture—as she is in indicating certain shadings that
imply a personification ("muffled linen," "sickly light," "deceit-

12 There are rhymes of
    ú-a with é-o, í-o, ó-a, ié-o
    é-a with ó-o, í-a
    í-a with í-e

ful cypress," "feverish fruit") and that project her own mood on things. The repetition of "mad," "demented," "insensate," "drunk" as qualifiers for very diverse beings and things of nature conveys a sense of strong, passionate, disordered movement.[13]

The past participle is also used as an adjective to qualify the result of an action. Most of the participles—and they are very numerous—allude to actions that undo, break, destroy, or consume things: "burned," "consumed," "divided," "pierced," "crushed," "choked," "flung down," "devoured." Since they almost always describe moral activities, they shed light upon the true meaning of the work's title. The anguish of earthly existence drains man as the wine press extracts the juice from the cluster of grapes, leaving them crushed and spent. The participle denotes the state that results from the cessation of action; the moment things and living beings strip themselves of their dynamics, they decay into death.

The poet prefers personification and simile to other kinds of imagery. Everything, even the material and the inert, is animated, personified, animalized, or vegetableized; everything can be expressed in terms of something else. The characteristic trait of this poetic cosmos is this incessant activity, the fluidity, the fusion of boundaries until they are completely erased.

There is a simile at every step. "Tree," "albatross," and "gulls" are the ideal terms of comparison that appear most repeatedly. The first simile is suggested by the analogy between the form of the tree and the circulatory system, between the tree's shade and moral anguish, and by the tree-Cross relationship. The second and third similes are suggested by the soaring, powerful, zigzagging flight of these sea birds; perhaps by the reading of Coleridge's "Ancient Mariner."

On occasion, there is a subtle, tender, delicate comparison:

Encargo a Blanca

Porque mi culpa fué la palabra.
Pero dame la tuya, la tuya
que era como paloma posada.
p. 15, lines 14–16.

---

13 "Mad cascade," "drunken albatross," "insensate waves," "demented flame," "mad tresses," "mad breath."

Request of Blanca

Because my sin was the word.
But give me yours, yours
So like a dove alight.

Or there is the fitting comparison between a moral, psychic
action and unrelieved, domestic chore:

La desásida

Mi voluntad la recojo
como ropa abandonada.
p. 64, lines 35–36.

The Forsaken One

I gather together my will
Like clothing carelessly strewn.

On occasion one finds a very intellectual comparison, based on
literary memories, like the one drawn between the doors and the
Cassandra of Aeschylus' *Agamemnon*.

On many occasions the simile adopts a fixed mode of expression not evident in the other books. It may be a combination of
(1) *a verb*, either in infinitive or conjugated form; (2) the
preposition "in"; (3) a *noun* alone or modified by one or several
adjectives:

cae en linda presa soltada.

she falls as beautiful prey set free.

en rápidas resinas se endurecía su habla.

her speech hardened as rapid resins.

arde en fucsias y dalias.

it burns as fuschias and dahlias.

entra en madre alborotada.

she enters as a mother alarmed.

In its final form, the comparative relationship is conveyed
through the adverb, which describes the verbal action and fulfills its logical function of being a complement of manner.

All of the stylistic characteristics described above reveal to us
the inner life of the poet, her conception of the world, the

ethical-religious roots that nourish her song. The images clarify and define her vision of the cosmos. *Wine Press* transports us to a complex world governed by imagination and memory. Its poems evoke sensory or mental objects, recreating and beautifying them through a play on their relationship to the rest of reality as it is perceived by the senses, the intelligence, and the memory. We look out on a ghost-like, hallucinated multitude of beings in motion, in continuous flux. We witness the transformation and dissolution of apparitions: for a moment they reveal their faces to us, they gesture to us, only to disintegrate immediately, like mist and foam. This vision corresponds exactly to Gabriela's spiritual state, to the delirium that rent her as she stood polarized between the here and the beyond, and to her resigned acceptance of death as a necessary and desirable end to the game and dream that is life.

The Transformation of Reality

BREAD (PAN) [1]

The poet sings of the discovery of a piece of bread on the table. This event, so apparently unimportant and trivial, takes on deep meaning as it is transformed and recreated into a poetic experience. The event is related in the form most suited to the narrative genre: a variation of the ballad. The verse lines are of nine, ten and eleven syllables, grouped into stanzas of four or six lines, the even lines joined by the same assonance. The eight-syllable model is not maintained. As is usual in this poetry, there is a preference for the nine-syllable line; an attempt is made to free the poem from its insistent meter by the combination of unequal meters without any formalistic concern. This lack of rigor produces an effect of carelessness and spontaneity that is very well suited to the domestic simplicity of the described event. The same effect is achieved by omitting the rhyme in the eighteenth line; the final word, *reconozco*, is not an assonant of *plato*, which precedes it in rhyming position:

> y no hay nadie tampoco en la casa
> sino este pan abierto en un plato,
> que con su cuerpo me reconoce
> y con el mío yo reconozco.
> *Felling*, p. 76, lines 15–18.

Nor is there anyone in the house
Save this opened bread upon a plate,

1 *Felling*, pp. 75–77.

> That with its body seems to know me
> And I with mine.

The unexpected omission, which surprises the reader, momentarily breaks the monorhyme and makes way for the retrospection that follows.

The groups of four lines generally combine nine, ten, or eleven syllables with a final line of another measure, thereby emphasizing the dramatic value. The six-line groups express the moments of most intense lyricism and subjectivity. When one reads the poem or listens to it, the ear captures, thanks to such details, the same expansion of rhythm found in the fluency of prose; it is a fluency that is very well suited to the note of spoken confidence that the poem imparts.

Within its very conciseness, the poem—hardly fifty lines long —includes four poetic "moments": the *evocation* of childhood and of other lands (three stanzas); the *finding* of the bread (four stanzas); the *communion* with the dead (two stanzas); the *communion* with the bread (two stanzas). The poem was inspired by an actual experience: it happened in Madrid. Gabriela was living as an exile in the midst of the barren Castilian countryside. The first four stanzas describe the poet's encounter with the bread, the first contact stirred by sensory perceptions of touch and smell. There, on the simple geometry of a pine table, bare of tablecloth, in the almost abstract silence, loneliness, and emptiness of a dining room, lies the piece of bread:

> *mitad quemado, mitad blanco,*
> *pellizcado encima y abierto*
> *en unos migajones de ampo.*
> p. 75, lines 2–4.

> Half of it burnt, half white,
> Pinched on the top and opened
> To its soft and snowy whiteness.

The description has the lineal purity, the play of planes and the sobriety of color one finds in a cubist still life. The poet comes closer to look at the bread, takes it in her hands, feels it, inhales its aroma, moved by the surprise of one who discovers an unknown object for the first time.

As in Proust's famous memories of the past, the familiar

texture and aroma plunge her into a dreamlike state that stimu-
lates memory and transforms sensations into recollections, into
nostalgias, into affection. Now the bread no longer smells like
bread; it smells like mother's milk, like the beloved valleys, like
the poet herself when she sings. These are the most beloved
things, those that have left the deepest, most decisive imprint on her spirit: the tenderness of her mother, the Elqui
valley, the land of Mexico, her own poetry. In the bare room
there is no other smell, there is no other presence. The poet and
the bread draw nearer to each other, they communicate. It is a
recognition that begins through purely physical means, through
smell, but which is enough to remove the poet from the present
and to envelop her in the world and images of the past.

The three following stanzas conjure up a parade of memories:
breads similar to this one, breads of Coquimbo, of Santiago, of
Oaxaca; those she ate in childhood when her fascinated child's
eyes saw in them the shape of a sun, of a fish, of a halo; bread
fresh from the oven, whose throbbing warmth, so like that of a
young pigeon, could be felt by the tender little hand. It is a
parade that summarizes much of Gabriela's psychology, facts
of her intimate being: her attachment to her corner of the earth,
her constant wandering from place to place, the vividness of
her childhood imagination, already inclined to metaphoric
vision, and the direct, inquisitive, impassioned dealing with
things.

The last stanza of this group brings us back once more to the
present, to "this day" in which, after a long period of forgetfulness,

> *los dos nos encontramos,*
> *yo, con mi cuerpo de Sara vieja*
> *y él con el suyo de cinco años.*
> p. 76, lines 28–30.

> The two of us did meet,
> I with my body of aged Sarah
> And he with his of five years of age.

What does the word "forgetfulness" mean here? It means that
in the years between that far off yesterday and the today the
bread was eaten mechanically, with the indifference of routine.

And now, this woman, old and sterile—like the Biblical Sarah—unsatisfied in her desire for motherhood, gazes at a bread as soft as a child of five, a symbol of life and fecundity, a symbol also of the love that binds those who share it together at the same table.

The reader may ask himself what blood ties, what secret sympathy bound Gabriela to the Hebrew people? In various places throughout her work there are poems dedicated to "The Sterile Woman" (*La mujer estéril*), to "Ruth, Moabite" (*Ruth, moabita*), to "Jewish Emigrant" (*Emigrada judía*); in others she calls herself Maccabee, Agar. She feels sterility as a curse; she sees in the act of sharing food an alliance of love and fidelity; she pays homage to the family dead whose invisible yet strongly felt presence determines many of her actions and words.

She converses with the dead at this moment of the poem; she turns it to let them feel the fragrance of this Castilian bread that is different yet the same one they all shared in other lands. As one who celebrates a rite to summon her spirits:

> Abro la miga y les doy su calor;
> lo volteo y les pongo su hálito.
>   p. 77, lines 37–38.

I open the bread and give them its warmth;
I turn it and lay before them its scent.

It is a communion that defies obstacles of time and space, of life and death. Hence the geographical and chronological specifications: "Castile," "in September ground," "in August reaped." Besides, in this special bread (from Castile, from the last harvest and oven batch), there beats the whole essence of *bread*, Its basic sameness, in spite of the diversity of its forms and origins, becomes symbolic of the oneness of the living and dead, of the love that masters time and reconciles differences, a oneness that permits us to glimpse the Absolute. One cannot ignore the religious assumptions in an analysis of this poem: the eucharist, the communion of the saints. The experience described and the atmosphere that permeates it is religious, ritualistic, almost mystic.

The two final stanzas contain the peak of the lyrical emotion that has been gradually growing in intensity to the rhythm of the verse lines. The poet, deeply moved, loses herself in the contemplation of the bread, in the loneliness of the house, in that silence so charged with inner life, with spiritual wealth, that it seems almost human. Repentant, she laments so many years of having forgotten the value and meaning of this object; finding it has infused her with a sense of purification, of the abundant fullness of life.

> entrego un llanto arrepentido
> por el olvido de tantos años,
> y la cara se me envejece
> o me renace en este hallazgo.
> p. 77, lines 41–44.

I abandon myself to repentant tears
For the forgetfulness of so many years,
And my face grows old
Or is reborn in this encounter.

The poem closes with a prayer for the continued communion of those who find each other again, until death.

From the point of view of artistic execution, the composition rests on two simple sensations, touch and smell, which stand out against the austere emptiness of a lonely house. These are the pillars of a complex edifice that fuses subtle materials of the most delicate spirituality: the life of childhood, filial love, friendship, nostalgia for one's homeland, remembrance of the dead, the cosmic emotion, the religious experience. The bread, personified and enveloped by the poet's astonishment, tenderness, and reverence, is at the expressive center, like the axis of this cosmos: a god that demands faithfulness, ritual, and an almost mystical meditation and union.

The images intensify this vision; they allude to unity in diversity:

> Huele a mi madre cuando dió su leche,
> huele a tres valles por donde he pasado:
> a Aconcagua, Pátzcuaro, a Elqui,
> y a mis entrañas cuando yo canto.
> p. 75, lines 9–12.

It smells of my mother when she gave her milk,
It smells of three valleys through which I have passed:

Aconcagua, Pátzcuaro, and Elqui,
And of my own womb when I sing.

Se ha comido en todos los climas
el mismo pan en cien hermanos.
                    p. 76, lines 19–20.

It has been eaten in all climes
The same bread in a hundred forms.

Es otro y es el que comimos
en tierras donde se acostaron.
                    p. 77, lines 35–36.

It is another and yet the same we ate
In lands in which they went to sleep.

Or, they reveal to us the poet's amazement at the eternal mystery
of things, their value as symbols of the eternal. These things
become a loving part of her deepest inner life, as they invite her
to the ecstasy of love and union.

Me parece nuevo o como no visto,
y otra cosa que él no me ha alimentado.
                    p. 75, lines 5 6.

It seems new to me as if never before seen
And as if it has never nourished me.

hasta que seamos otra vez uno
y nuestro día haya acabado . . .
                    p. 77, lines 49–50.

Until we once again are one
And our day has ended.

With extreme simplicity and transparency of words, with a
calculated economy of rhetorical devices and an intentional
casualness of form, the poet leads us into this corner of delicate
intimacy, of absorbed meditation, of mystery. The "realism" of
this vision, her ability to make the artistic technique seem natural
and alive, remind one of the prodigious spontaneity of some of
Cervantes' pages or the penetrating, wise look of Velásquez'
"Meninas!" Like them, Gabriela possesses the Hispanic gift for
capturing the concrete, impressionistic vision of reality; like the

Mystics, she has the ability to transcend the apparent and intuit the hidden Absolute present in all things. Perhaps the reason for her song, the idea that governs its poetic world is, as here, the discovery of the divine in all earthly things; thus, death's hold over living creatures can now be broken.

"TREE, SON" (*HIJO ÁRBOL*) [2]

The silhouette of the winter tree is clearly etched against the blue of the sky; the poet recalls that portrait of "Erasmus of Rotterdam," painted by Hans Holbein the younger, which she has seen so many times in the galleries of the Louvre. Against a background of dark draperies, the painter has outlined the firm contour of the Humanist's pensive head. In that noble profile he has emphasized the long sensitive nose, the eyes half opened in a frown of meditation, the hand on the verge of committing his thoughts to paper. The gesture of the hand, the finely etched lines of the mouth barely hint at the intense psychic dynamism of the figure. The tree captures in its smooth, clear surface this fleeting moment, in which the tension of spiritual energies is about to channelize itself into moral, intellectual, or physical action.

The relationship between this portrait and the tree motivates the sonnet, "Tree, Son" (*Hijo árbol*). The poet discloses this when she repeats it at the beginning and end of the octave.

> *El arbol invernal se estampa sobre*
> *el cielo azul, como el perfil de Erasmo*
> *de Rotterdam, absorto por el pasmo*
> *de su dureza y enjutez de cobre.*
>
> *Más noble así que si estuviera vivo*
> *de frondazón sensual, con su severa*
> *forma que aguarda la ancha primavera*
> *en su perfil de Erasmo pensativo.*
> pp. 113–14, lines 1–8.

Against the sky of blue
Stands the winter tree embossed

[2] From "Sonnets of Pruning" (*Sonetos de la poda*) in *Wine Press*, pp. 113–14.

Like the face of Erasmus of Rotterdam, in wonder lost
At its hard dryness of copper hue.

More noble thus than with living crown
Of sensual green, its form severe
Waiting for Spring's fullness to draw near
Etched like Erasmus' pensive frown.

Out of this simile, as from an intricate knot, there runs the complex net of allusions and analogies that make of "Tree, Son" (*Hijo árbol*) one of the most elegant and elaborate poems in *Wine Press*.

The metric form deviates very little from the classical norm, but its rigor is diminished by some licenses that impart a certain naturalness to it: the placement of *sobre* (on) in a final position of rhyme; the appearance of the third and fourth rhymes within the octave; the abundance of overflow lines; the harsh melody of the penultimate line. The sonnet, like the act of pruning, imposes on the subject matter those patterns that satisfy the demands of the spirit.

There are two parts: the octave, which describes the tree; the sextain, which describes the act of pruning. All the details and the careful choice of vocabulary justify the view that the poet's point of departure is the comparison with Holbein's "Erasmus." The tree is *etched* against the sky as is the profile of the humanist lost in "wonder at its hardness and coppery dryness." These are also qualities we discover in the subject of the portrait, in the sharp nose, prominent cheek bones, muscles tensed by mental effort, qualities that describe the psychology behind the figure as well.

The first lines of the sonnet trace the outline of a landscape: a strong, copper-colored trunk against the blue of the sky; a sober contrast of color, a firm, sure sketch. In the second quatrain, the speculative comparison is drawn between the dry trunk and a tree in the fullness of its vitality and verdure. The poet claims to prefer the sober nakedness of the winter tree to the sensual foliage of Springtime; it is a preference determined by a value judgment that sets ethical considerations above aesthetic ones. At the end of the octave, subtle analogies are drawn between this tree "that awaits the fullness of spring" and the meditative abstraction of Erasmus, which is a prelude to the wealth of ideas he is about to set down on paper. The adjective "pensive" that is added to the simile at this point underlines the closeness of the relationship between the two objects that are being compared.

In the terzets the poet speaks of pruning the tree:

> con amargo brío
> por darle gesto como a un hijo mío
> hasta que se me vuelva criatura.
>
> Y al cielo que bosteza de su hastío
> y al paisaje sin escalofrío
> lo entrego como norma de amargura.
>
>   p. 114, lines 9–14.

> with bitter force
> to give it form as to a son of mine
> until it should become my child.
>
> And to the heavens who yawn in weariness
> And to the countryside of tremors shorn
> I offer it as a norm of bitterness.

"But I prune it with bitter force"—any action of the spirit upon matter, any act of culture and cultivation forces us to limit, to amputate, to channel the free and powerful creative energies of nature; such processes—necessary though they may be—always bring us pain. As he meditates, Erasmus organizes his ideas, rejects those that do not suit his purposes; when we prune a tree we modify its form and we channel its growth and development according to our own discretion. The poet wants to give the tree expression, to transform it into something of her own making, to take possession of it as a mother would. Pruning is like educating a child. The necessary severity pains one as much as the slashes that reverberate on the heart of the tree. And this resemblance, born of the poet's recollection of the pedagogical value of Erasmus' work, is the key to the poem's title "Tree, Son" (*Hijo árbol*).

The final terzet again draws our gaze to the now humanized background and landscape: a blue, monotonous sky that "yawns in its boredom," a landscape without life, without a tremor. To these (to life and duty?) the poet offers the pruned tree, as

Erasmus will offer to the empty pages before him his thoughts filled with the bitter science of living.

The predominant concept of the sonnet is the dramatic cleavage between matter and spirit, between nature and culture. Its melancholy, austere language reveals to us the secret attraction that nature's freedom holds for the poet, the bitterness of all her renunciations. The rationality and lineal clarity of the artistic form is consistent with the moral sense implicit in the lines. Gabriela's art has never before come so close to the moderation and serenity of classicism as here. The last line closes the sonnet masterfully, in the manner of the most expert sonnet writers. The sharp and fitting concept expresses better than any other the internal justification of all of Mistral's poetry:

> *lo entrego como norma de amargura.*

> I offer it as a norm of bitterness.

PANAMANIAN *TAMBORITO* DANCE
(*TAMBORITO PANAMEÑO*) [3]

The happy, untamed Panamanian national dance is the inspiration for this lovely poem. The last line of the traditional song that accompanies the dance is repeated as a refrain at the end of almost all the stanzas. The poet's attention is focused on the "happiness" of the drum, on her own desire to abandon herself to the dance, which she expresses in the language of the people:

Panameño, panameño,	Panamanian, Panamanian,
panameño de mi vida,	Panamanian of my life,
yo quiero que tú me lleves	I want you to take me
al tambor de la alegría.	To the drum of happiness.

These two details are the key to the poetic vision.

The metric pattern faithfully reproduces the rhythm of the dance: couplets of four eight-syllable lines, assonance of the even lines, the odd lines, free. The accentuated rhythm, marvel-

3 *Felling*, pp. 119–21.

ously exact, suggests the passionate movements of the dance. In order to lessen the monotony and insistence of the refrain, she employs a variety of modulations; among these is the omission of the refrain in the third and sixth couplets, as well as a slight alteration with each repetition. The transposition of the musical rhythm to the rhythm of words is one of the most beautiful achievements of the poem. Its stanzas could well be sung to the beat of the dance, thanks to the authenticity of its graceful folkloric air.

The composition is organized into two units of five stanzas each. The first five describe the dance; the last five speak of its effect on the dancers. The spell of the *tamborito* carries us back to the past; in its rhythms there vibrates the irresistible call of the jungle and of blood.

"Panamanian *Tamborito* Dance" belongs to the group of American poems in *Felling*. Gabriela's Americanism is always tinged with a strong Indianism. She feels that the essence of America, its originality, its uniqueness, is to be found in its indigenous element. Her love for the land, the landscapes, the towns, the people, and the objects of these countries is always accompanied by nostalgia for the pre-Columbian past, by her admiration for the Inca, Maya, and Aztec cultures. These are combined with a protest against conquerors and agents, a genuine social and pedagogical interest, and a great sympathy and compassion for the conditions of the Indians today. In her poems she offers us an idealized vision of the Indian and his culture. This idealization is partly literary in origin and partly due to personal ideology and psychology, though the latter are not too clear. They may spring from the embers of anti-Spanish animosity and her personal suspicion of a society based on race.

The preoccupation—almost the obsession—with the value of the Indian as a dominant element in Hispanic-American culture leads the poet to attribute an indigenous origin to the *tamborito* dance. In reality, its variations of rhythm against a background of sustained monotony seems to be typical of African cultures; on the other hand, the dancers' costumes and some of their postures and steps doubtlessly reflect Spanish influence. The *tamborito* may be a product of the crossing of three races that met and fused on the American continent.

The poem begins with the beautiful evocation of the nocturnal landscape of the isthmus, rent by the beats of the drum:

De una parte mar de espejos,	To one side, a sea of
de la otra serranía,	mirrors,
y partiéndonos la noche	To the other mountain range,
el tambor de la alegría.	And cutting across the night
	The drum of happiness.
Donde es bosque de quebracho,	
panamá y especiería,	Where there is quebracho
apuñala de pasión	forest,
el tambor de la alegría.	Panama hat and grocery,
p. 119, lines 1–8.	There stabs with passion
	The drum of happiness.

Within this evocation one finds the beautiful visual image "sea of mirrors" (of euphuistic flavor), the majestic, tropical trees of hard, aromatic wood, the plastic force of the expression "stabs with passion," with which she initiates the personification of the *tamborito.* Its spirited rhythm stands out against a somber, shining, and perfumed background of night. In the third stanza the *tamborito* becomes a sorcerer presiding over pagan rites:

Emboscado silbador,	Ambushed whistler
cebo de la hechicería,	Calling to witchcraft,
guiño de la media noche,	Wink of midnight,
panameña idolatría.	Panamanian idolatry.
p. 119, lines 9–12.	

The poet exalts its enslaving seduction, the manner in which it insinuates itself upon the senses, ensnares the instinct, overpowers one through surprise and cunning. The two final stanzas of this part describe the musical instrument as well: its increasingly intense and excited tom-tom, like the breathless respiration of those who suffer from altitude sickness:

Los muñones son caoba
y la piel venadería,
y más loco a cada tumbo
el tambor de la alegría.

Jadeante como pecho
que las sierras subiría,
y la noche que se funde
del tambor de la alegría.
p. 120, lines 13–20.

The limbs are mahogany
And the skin of deer hide made,
And wilder yet with every crash
The drum of happiness.

Breathless as a heart that has
Scaled mountain ridges high,
And the night that is fused
With the drum of happiness.

The two final lines in this last stanza correspond symmetrically
to the two in the first stanza. In the latter, the nocturnal silence is suddenly torn by the first, energetic beats of the drum:

y partiéndonos la noche   And rending the night
el tambor de la alegría.   The drum of happiness.
            lines 3–4.

In the former, the night itself has surrendered to the sorcery of
the dance:

y la noche que se funde   And the night that is fused
del tambor de la alegría.   With the drum of happiness.
            lines 19–20.

The five stanzas of the second part form the response of the
dancers—Hispano-Americans and the poet among them—to the
call of the dance; thus, the use of verbs and pronouns in the first
person plural and the apostrophe, "you," which gives our assent.
The desire expressed in the traditional couplet

yo quiero que tú me lleves   I want you to take me
al tambor de la alegría.   To the drum of happiness.

is substituted for the assertive categorical "We go," which denotes the transformation of the wish into the act. The use of
the diminutive form modifies the refrain and communicates the
full, joyful, loving consent, the breaking of resistance:

> *Vamos donde tú nos quieres;*
> *que era donde nos querías,*
> *embozado de las greñas,*
> *tamborito de la alegría.*
> p. 12, lines 21–24.

We go where you want us to
Where once before you wanted us,

> Concealed in the tangled reeds
> Little drum of happiness.

The two stanzas that follow refer to the indigenous origin of the dance—dance of the red-skinned people—and to its power to awaken ancestral memories:

> *vamos como quien se acuerda*
> *al tambor de la alegría.*
> p. 120, lines 27–28.

> We go as one who remembers
> To the little drum of happiness.

As we respond to the dance we are returned once more to the bosom of our native race and culture, as a child once lost avidly seeks the breast of its mother. We had been torn from the warmth of our native culture by the "pirate sea, Phoenician sea," by the greed and evil cunning of the merchants who sought new routes for commerce with the East Indies. But the *tamborito* "steals us from the thief" and returns us to paganism. It is a return effected without a path because it need only follow "the clash and beat" of this rhythm, which, according to the poet, nullifies in Hispano-Americans the effects of European, Christian civilization.

In "Panamanian *Tamborito* Dance" Gabriela reveals to us her pagan face. Here she sings of the spell of the American jungle, of the tropical night, the sensual intoxication of a rhythm that magnetizes, that loosens the restraints of reason, and that makes the body and mind surrender to the physical joy of movement, to the ritualistic purposes implicit in the dance.

The vocabulary and images blend into the poetic thought with plastic and evocative power: they speak of the character and powers attributed to the dance. "Mad," "fever," "clash," "palpitation," "passion," "stab" describe its growing, intense frenzy. "Hidden in the tangled reeds," "call to witchery," "ambushed whistler," "wink of midnight" allude to its powers of seduction, to its irresistible authority. The splendid metaphor "red milk" reveals the affectionate values that come into play when Gabriela speaks of the Indians, of the Americas, the fertile and liberating virtue she attributes to their ethnic influence. Beneath it all, perhaps subconsciously, one senses the opposition nature-culture, and the nostalgia for the simple, natural life felt by a soul that has always felt very close to the earth, to all that is undefiled by civilization. Indigenous things are for Gabriela what the "village" as opposed to the "capital" was for our classic authors and for the naturalistic idealism of the Renaissance.

LAND OF ABSENCE
(*PAIS DE LA AUSENCIA*) [4]

The theme of nostalgia, of what Gabriela prefers to call by its more precise, richer, Portuguese name *saudade* (longing), is one of the most repeated and important poetic themes in her work. She lived almost all of her life in the close spiritual climate of longing, as she wandered continuously far from the places, persons, and things she loved. Those things were always present in her memory, so close within her that she seemed to have them within arm's reach; they were the content of all her dreams and fantasies.

Confronted by her determined memory, time and space vanished. To go back in time, to move her spirit from one space to another, was almost a daily habit of hers. Many times, in conversation with people, she would give the impression of withdrawing and losing herself; of momentarily leaving behind all that surrounded her and becoming absorbed in some far-off contemplation and of returning, suddenly, to the here and now, with the happy or sorrowful imprints of that inner experience still fresh on her face. This would explain much of her forgetfulness and distraction.

She lived, so to speak, on a level that seemed to negate the realities of space, time, forgetfulness, death. She had found happiness and a liberating refuge in recollection and poetic fantasy. Yet, although it may seem contradictory, she was not an escapist; she did not flee from the present nor from the realities that surrounded her. She felt their palpable presence with complete intensity; she loved them and delighted in them with possessive, passionate, maternal tenderness. One of the distinctive traits of her poetic vision is realism. Each thing she had

4 *Felling*, pp. 125–27.

lived, physically or spiritually, was of tremendous importance to her. Through that realism she hoped to preserve them all—even the past and distant ones—in the here and now. Some she retained in their visible, tangible form; others were evoked and enveloped in a halo of nostalgia. This explains her going and coming from the past to the present, from the here to the there; one can understand the anguish she expressed in one of her poems when she discovered the havoc that forgetfulness was wreaking on her memory.

"Land of Absence" (*País de la ausencia*) expresses better than any of the other poems of similar theme the value that the past, the distant, and the lost had for the poet. It shows with what clarity and precision of words she could give concreteness to the abstract, to psychic realities. It is a self-analysis of such delicacy and sharpness that at certain moments it recalls the sharp lyricism of Becquer.

The subject of the poem is the description of the "land of absence," an imaginary place created by the poet, and so real that she can give us the most minute details about it.

The meter is of the most faultless regularity. The stanzas consist of six-syllable lines joined together by assonantal rhyme on the last syllable of the even lines. There are seven stanzas of eight, six, and ten lines, combined with a certain symmetry: 8-8-8-8-8-10-8. Significantly, the longest stanza, the next to last, contains the enumeration of all the things lost by the poet, those that, as they are remembered, form the land of absence. The refrain,

y en país sin nombre	And in land without name
me voy a morir,	I am going to die.

closes the second, the fourth, and the seventh stanzas, repeating itself at almost regular intervals. The first time, it closes the description of the country; the second time, altered to

y es mi patria donde	And my land is where
vivir y morir,	I live and die,

it expresses the certainty that, in spite of its fictitious, dreamlike character, this country is her true land. The last repetition brings the poem emphatically to a close.

The refrain reveals the poet's oscillation between the two

different levels of reality: actual countries like Chile, Mexico, Spain, in which she engages in her daily work; and, at the same time, the ideal country, the country "without a name," where she lives her true life, the one that is really important to her.

The brevity of the six-syllable lines, the sharpness of the accentuated "íes" of the assonance give the poem a rapid, murmuring, winged rhythm that underlines the poetic intent with maximum efficacy and beauty. It creates in the reader a kind of drowsiness, a laxness similar to that which accompanies moods of nostalgia and daydreaming.

Within the tight, internal unity of the poem, one can distinguish a division, though not very pronounced. The first four stanzas describe what this country *is* and what *it is not*. The last three tell how it was made, what things went into its formation.

The first stanza conveys its strangeness, the way in which it differs from ordinary countries. The images point to its lack of physical form, the absence of time, its lack of color:

más ligero que ángel	Lighter than angel
y señal sutil,	And of feature vague,
color de alga muerta,	Color of dead algae,
color de neblí,	The color of hawk,
con edad de siempre,	The age of forever,
sin edad feliz.	Without happy age.

  p. 125, lines 3–8.

They also point to the absence of blue heavens and seas, of flowers and fruit:

No echa granada,	It bears no pomegranates,
no cría jazmín,	It yields no jasmine,
y no tiene cielos	And it has no heavens
ni mares de añil.	Nor indigo seas.

  lines 9–14.

It would be interesting to study a selection of the terms of comparison: "angel," a disembodied spirit; "subtle feature," vague indication; "dead algae," colorless, languid; "hawk" whose swift flight makes it impossible for one to see the color of its plumage. These objects, in spite of their random grouping (angel, feature, plant, bird), have in common swiftness, lightness, absence of color. They evoke that which escapes perception by the senses. The series leaves an impression of something barely glimpsed because of its lightness and evanescence.

The country is sterile and without palpable beauty: it does not yield the juicy spendor of the pomegranate, nor the fragrant and delicate jasmine; it has no skies of intense blue; no one knows it; it is never named.

Nombre suyo, nombre	Its name, its name
nunca se lo oí.	Never have I heard it.
lines 15–16.	

The serial enumeration of negative qualities heightens this ideal, specialized nature. The descriptive method consists of the contrast between countries of actual geography and the imaginary one. The latter is defined as a negation of the former.

The two stanzas that follow detail new peculiarities. It is impossible to get to the country either by bridge or boat; the poet did not discover it nor was she seeking it.

Parece una fábula,	It seems a fable
que yo me aprendí,	That I have learned,
sueño de tomar	A dream of taking
y de desasir.	And letting go.
p. 126, lines 23–26.	

But in spite of its being formless and nameless, it is the only place in which the poet lives and dies!

We detect an elegiac, melancholy note in the language. Gabriela seems to be moving in a void, grasping at elusive images, fantasies born of her sorrow for all that is forever lost. The palpable world, the real countries, no longer matter to her, no longer have any meaning. Only this illusory country fills her heart.

In the fifth and sixth stanzas, she speaks of the things that have fashioned the imaginary place: lands she once had and has now lost, creatures who have died, that which one was hers and which has abandoned her. The elegiac tone, very tense, lays bare the wound and, as always occurs in literary elegy, the evocation—the *ubi sunt*—creates the illusion of momentarily recapturing in all of its warm beauty the many things that have been lost.

Perdí cordilleras	I lost mountain ranges
en donde dormí;	Where I once did sleep;
perdí huertos de oro	I lost golden orchards
dulces de vivir;	With living sweet;
perdí yo las islas	I lost the islands
de caña y añil	Of cane and azure deep
y las sombras de ellas	And as their shadows merged
me las ví ceñir	I did see
y juntas y amantes	Them together and loving
hacerse país.	Form a land for me.

pp. 126–27,
lines 37–46.

The emphatic repetition of "I lost" at the beginning of each unit of the series and the use of the first person singular in the verbs and pronouns make the memory more dramatic, more intensely felt. The reader is moved by the strong subjectivity of the passage. The poet lives from the union of these "loving shadows" that cluster tightly together and offer themselves to her as the only possible dwelling place.

In the last stanza, these objects, so beautiful and so beloved, evaporate, dissolve, become spectral and fluid:

Guedejas de nieblas	Long locks of mist
sin dorso y cerviz,	Disembodied and free,
alientos dormidos	Sleeping breaths following
me los ví seguir,	I did see
y en años errantes	And through wandering years
volverse país.	Formed a land for me.

lines 47–52.

Transformed into mist, into creatures of illusion and memory, they accompany the author faithfully in her wandering through the world—her only loyal companions until her death.

Unlike conventional elegy, the lament for the things lost and the philosophical consolation are omitted in this poem. The poem sings of the bitterness of living only on shadows, without apparent hope. Gabriela could be called "dweller of the mists," as Bécquer once referred to himself. She fought to save matter from death and time, to place it in a purer dimension, one free of limitations. This subtle concept of a world of ideal objects nourished by the spirit produces a delicate, purified lyricism. As we read "Land of Absence" (*País de la ausencia*), we know we are touching the essence of Mistral's vision of reality and of its transformation into a work of art.

Nocturne *(Nocturno)*

AN ANALYSIS of Gabriela Mistral's work will always present serious difficulties to anyone who attempts to study it rigorously. The one who undertakes such a task will not be able to ignore the intimate relationship between the themes of the poetry and the life of the poet. From the data contained in the published biographies, he will have to separate, very delicately, what is true from what is a product of the imaginative enthusiasm of her biographers. Even when reading Gabriela's own accounts of her life, he will have to tear away the mask of fiction she wore to shield herself from the impertinent or malevolent curiosity of the world. Perhaps in her mature years, when she was more serene, she attempted to temper, through ambiguity, the almost brutal frankness of her first book, *Desolation*.

However, the biographical elements in her verses neither diminish the beauty of the fiction nor the quality and skill of the art with which she has transfigured reality "Nocturne" (*Nocturno*) from *Desolation* can be used as an example.

> *¡Padre nuestro que estás en los cielos,*
> *por qué te has olvidado de mí!*
> *Te acordaste del fruto en febrero,*
> *al llagarse su pulpa rubí.*
> *¡Llevo abierto también mi costado,*
> *y no quieres mirar hacia mí!*
>
> *Te acordaste del negro racimo,*
> *y lo diste al lagar carmesí;*
> *y aventaste las hojas de álamo,*
> *con tu aliento, en el aire sutil.*

¡Y en el ancho lagar de la muerte
aún no quieres mi pecho exprimir!

Caminando vi abrir las violetas;
el falerno del viento bebí,
y he bajado, amarillos, mis párpados,
por no ver más enero ni abril.
Y he apretado la boca, anegada
de la estrofa que no he de exprimir,
¡Has herido la nube de otoño
y no quieres volverte hacia mí!

Me vendió él que besó mi mejilla;
me negó por la túnica ruín.
Yo en mis versos el rostro con sangre,
como Tú sobre el paño, le dí
y en mi noche del Huerto, me han sido
Juan cobarde y el Angel hostil.

Ha venido el cansancio infinito
a clavarse en mis ojos, al fin:
el cansancio del día que muere
y el del alba que debe venir;
¡el cansancio del cielo de estaño
y el cansancio del cielo de añil!

Ahora suelto la mártir sandalia
y las trenzas pidiendo dormir.
y perdida en la noche, levanto
el clamor aprendido de Ti:
¡Padre nuestro que estás en los cielos,
por qué te has olvidado de mí!
                    Desolation, pp. 116–17.

Our Father who art in heaven,
Why hast Thou forsaken me!
Thou did'st remember the February fruit,
When torn was its pulp of ruby.
My side is pierced also
Yet Thou will'st not look at me!

Thou did'st remember the dark grape cluster
And did'st give it to the crimsoned press,
And Thou did'st fan the poplar leaves
With thy breath of gentleness.
Yet in the deep wine press of death
Thou still would'st not my heart express!

As I walked I saw violets open;
And I drank the wine of the wind,

And I have lowered my yellowed eyelids
Never more to see Winter or Spring.
And I have tightened my mouth to stifle
The verses I am never to sing.
Thou hast wounded the cloud of Autumn
And Thou will'st not turn toward me!

I was sold by the one who kissed my cheek;
He betrayed me for the tunic vile.
I gave him in my verses, my blood-stained face,
As Thine imprinted on her veil,
And in my night of the Orchard I have found
John reluctant and the Angel hostile.

And now an infinite fatigue
Has come to pierce my eyes:
The fatigue of the day that is dying
And of the dawn that will arise;
The fatigue of the sky of metal
The fatigue of indigo skies!

And now I loosen my martyred sandal
And my locks, for I am longing to sleep.
And lost in the night, I lift my voice
In the cry I have learned from Thee:
Our Father who art in heaven,
Why hast Thou forsaken me!

No other poem of hers is so faithful to the facts, or expresses
more beautifully the spiritual turmoil caused within her by the
betrayal of her beloved and his marriage to another. It is one
of the most beautiful poems of *Desolation*, one of the most
Mistralian in theme and style. It records the disillusion of sec
ond love and it voices the anguish, the clamor for death. But
art has so sublimated the personal element that the reader finds
in "Nocturne" not the individual, usual case of a betrayal of
love but the representation of all human sorrow in its most
solitary, most inescapable moment.

THE TITLE.

The title has no musical connotation. It denotes the identity
night-sorrow, of age-old use in world literature.

> *y perdida en la noche levanto*
> *el clamor aprendido de Ti.*
>   lines 35–36.

> and lost in the night I lift my voice
> in the cry I have learned from Thee.

In addition to this, however, her use of the image "and in my night of the Orchard" underlines the poet's identification with Christ. It is possible that Gabriela may also have been influenced by José Asunción Silva's "Nocturne," which she admired so much. Other nocturnes—"The Defeat" (*La derrota*), "The Consummation" (*La consumación*), and "Old Weavers" (*Tejedores viejos*) of *Felling*—are very similar in mood to the poem here under discussion. They and the "Nocturne" form a link between one book and the other.

METRIC PATTERN

In addition to the similarity of mood, these poems share identical rhythmic patterns: stanzas of six ten-syllable lines, with assonance on the last syllable of the even lines. It is a monotonous rhythm, strengthened by repetitions and parallelisms of phrases and lines. Such a meter could easily degenerate into simple singsong if, as in the "Nocturne," the lines were not interlaced with exclamations that rise like cries above the murmur of the psalmody. There is perfect compatibility between the metric form and the artistic intent: the "Nocturne" is a prayer fashioned on the pattern of the psalms. The first versicle from The Lord's Prayer and part of the first one from the Twenty-first Psalm—with a slight variation—open and close the poem in the style of a refrain:

> *¡Padre nuestro que estás en los cielos*
> *por qué te has olvidado de mí!*
> lines 1–2.

> Our Father who art in heaven
> Why hast Thou forsaken me?

The refrain frames the prayer in the same way that the chants do the psalms. We now discover the true meaning of the poem's title: "nocturne" is the name given to each of the three parts of the matins prayer in the divine service. Unlike a monk, however, the poet does not rise to praise God at midnight; sleepless and grieved, she hurls her imprecation from the night of her abandonment and helplessness.

In the carefully constructed composition we distinguish two thought units, each of which contains three stanzas. The third stanza, which closes the first unit, is the longest of all: eight lines instead of the six required by the metric pattern. This variation marks the division between the two units.

The first unit develops the theme of divine forgetfulness by the serial enumeration of four parallel phrases, similar in content and syntactical structure. These cover the three initial stanzas. Each phrase includes its antithesis: Thou did'st remember all things; Thou will'st not remember me.

> *Te acordaste del fruto en febrero*
> *. . . y no quieres mirar hacia mí.*

> Thou did'st remember the February fruit
> . . . yet Thou will'st not look at me!

> *Te acordaste del negro racimo,*
> *aventaste las hojas del álamo*
> *. . . y aun no quieres mi pecho exprimir.*

> Thou did'st remember the black grape cluster,
> Thou did'st fan the poplar leaves
> . . . yet Thou would'st not my heart express.

> *Has herido la nube de otoño*
> *. . . y no quieres volverte hacia mí.*

> Thou hast wounded the cloud of autumn
> and Thou will'st not turn toward me!

The reiteration of this reproach produces an effect of mounting intensity and reveals to us the poet's intention of dramatizing her absolute abandonment and exclusion, through the will of God, from the norm that governs all of creation.

Although He is called Father, the God of the "Nocturne" bears more resemblance to the powerful, terrible Jehovah of the Old Testament than to the one of the Christian revelation. The poet demands that His destructive force annihilate her in the same way that he ripens the fruit, wrings the juice from the cluster of grapes in the wine press, fans the dry leaves and

dissolves the cloud of autumn. At the root of this conception
—which has a considerable pagan element—there throbs the
rebellious protest against pain, the thirst for annihilation. The
poet feels that God has abandoned her and pictures him movingly as an implacable and hostile power.

With supreme artistry she has chosen for the series of contrasts four objects already approaching the terminal point of
their seasonal cycle: fruit in February,[5] the black grape cluster,
the dry leaf, the autumn cloud. The adjectives of color in the
hues of ruby, crimson, and black evoke the image of blood. The
poet claims that "her side is also pierced," in the same way
that the fruit already shows the first signs of its approaching
decomposition.

The first line of the third stanza interrupts the series with an
impassioned evocation of the sensory beauty and intoxication
of the world. For but a moment we glimpse the ardent pleasure
of the senses, the impetus of the creative and positive forces of
life and the spirit, only to return immediately to the obsessive
insistence of the final antithesis:

> *Caminando vi abrir las violetas,*
> *el falerno del viento bebí,*
> *y he bajado, amarillos, mis párpados,*
> *por no ver más enero ni abril;*
> *y he apretado mi boca, anegada,*
> *de la estrofa que no he de exprimir.*
> *Has herido la nube de Otoño*
> *y no quieres volverte hacia mí.*
>   lines 12–20.

As I walked I saw violets open,
And I drank the wine of the wind,
And I have lowered my yellowed eyelids,
Never more to see Winter or Spring;
And I have tightened my mouth to stifle
The verses I am never to sing.
Thou hast wounded the cloud of Autumn
And Thou will'st not turn toward me!

The contrast between the autumnal images of ripening harvest
and rain and the spring images of flowering and Dionysian vi-

5 February in Chile is the height of summer.

tality is very effectively drawn in this passage. But the poet closes her eyes to the tenderness of the violets and stifles the song that rushes to her lips.

The very Mistralian vocabulary of this first part is characterized by an intense realism that recalls the plastic style of the Spanish baroque writers: "to wound oneself," "the pierced side," "black cluster," "to wring," "I have stifled," "yellow eyelids," "fruit," "pulp," "wine press," "you fanned," "leaves," "wounded"; they are words that originate in rural, agricultural experiences. The vocabulary of the second part derives from the poet's intention to compare her personal sorrow with the passion of Christ. They are all strong, concrete, expressive words intended for descriptions of violence and death.

The fourth stanza, the first of the second thought-unit, describes the cause of the sorrow with forceful images: it is a true passion that almost literally repeats the passion of the Lord. We note the rapidity with which the facts are narrated, the abundance and expressive force of the verbs all in the preterite tense:

> Me vendió el que besó mi mejilla,
> me negó por la túnica ruín.
> Yo en mis versos el rostro con sangre,
> como Tú, sobre el paño, le dí,
> y en mi noche del Huerto me han sido
> Juan cobarde y el Angel hostil.
> lines 21–26.

> I was sold by the one who kissed my cheek,
> He betrayed me for the tunic vile.
> I gave him in my verses, my blood-stained face,
> as Thine imprinted on her veil,
> And in my night of the Orchard I have found
> John reluctant and the Angel hostile.

It is a stanza brimming with biographical allusions, with keys that depict the experience and its consequences on her spirit. Taken together with the refrain that frames the poem, it becomes quite clear that the analogy with the passion of Christ is the point of departure for this poem. More precisely, all of the "Nocturne" is a variation, a kind of mental projection, only partially explicit, of the first lines of the Twenty-first Psalm,

"My Lord, my Lord, why hast Thou forsaken me? Thou art far from my prayers, from the words of my cry." These words, spoken by the Lord upon the cross, enable us to see the unfathomable depths of nothingness to which the Savior descends, with full awareness and complete liberty, in order that men may be redeemed. The poet, also crucified, knows something of that abyss; from its depths she calls out to the Father with the same anguished and mighty cry. This first analogy contains the others within it: the image "my side is also pierced," of the first stanza; "my night of the Orchard"; "I was sold by the one who kissed by cheek"; "he betrayed me for the tunic vile"; "In my verses, my blood-stained face."

There is an extremely important detail that differentiates the second part of the poem from the first. The poet no longer speaks to the Father, the First Person of the Holy Trinity. She now turns to the Son and speaks to him in intimate conversation, as if she were reflecting on her personal situation and comparing it to the Passion. By virtue of this change, her human anguish is transfigured and sweetened in union with the Redeemer. The rebellious, almost defiant, imprecation is followed by the humble entreaty, free from bitterness, modulated and moderated by fatigue. The entire poem thus takes on a profoundly Christian sense. The stanza upon which we are commenting appears at the moment of maximum tension and lyricism.

The anticlimax immediately begins with the fifth stanza. Here the poet speaks to us of her fatigue, of that total exhaustion that follows all crises, acting as a psychological respite. In the first line, the image "to pierce my eyes, finally" still follows from the comparisons with the Passion. The exclamation "finally" indicates relief from the spiritual tension. One hears something like a deep sigh in the new series of four parallel constructed lines, with their comparisons of past and future, summer and winter:

> el cansancio del día que muere
> y el del alba que debe venir;
> ¡y el cansancio del cielo de estaño
> y el cansancio del cielo de añil!
>   lines 29–32.

> The fatigue of the day that is dying
> And of the dawn that will arise;
> And the fatigue of the sky of metal
> And the fatigue of indigo skies!

We should view this stanza as the symmetric opposite of the third stanza of the first part. There, the poet felt the call of life, of beauty and of song, but by an effort of will she rejected it, in rebellious protest. Here, indifference invades her; nothing attracts her, nothing is capable of freeing her from her endless fatigue. She could say, inverting Kempis' phrase: Life, where is thy sting?

The metaphor "life—road" reappears in the first and third lines of the last stanza:

> *Ahora suelto la mártir sandalia*
> *y las trenzas pidiendo dormir*
> *y perdida en la noche levanto*
> *el clamor aprendido de Tí.*
> lines 33–36.

> And now I loosen my martyred sandal
> And my locks, for I am longing to sleep
> And lost in the night, I lift my voice
> In the cry I have learned from Thee.

In the third stanza, as we have seen, the comparison made way for a tender and beautiful digression among rough images of consummation. Now it awakens in the poet a longing for rest, for lying peacefully in the sleep of death. She no longer invokes the inflexible law that consumes all things in time; she clamors at the doors of the Son's heart and surrenders, helpless, to his mercy. The lines, "and lost in the night, I life my voice/In the cry I have learned from thee," denote a closer bond with God, a confidence greater than the questions and reproaches of the first part of the poem.

The "Nocturne" summarizes the main themes of Gabriela Mistral's poetry: God, love, sorrow, death, the scorn of the world, the search for the eternal. As in any romantic form, she lays bare the subjective experience without reticence, without minimizing it; she expresses overwhelming emotions. Her sources are perhaps too human, too deeply felt, too sensual, and each line, as it springs forth, seems to leave a fresh imprint of tears and blood.

> Yo en mis versos, el rostro con sangre
> como Tú, sobre el paño, le dí.

> I in my verses, with blood-stained face,
> As Thine imprinted on her veil.

In the "Artist's Decalogue" (*Decálogo del Artista*), Gabriela had said: "You will bring forth your work as a son is brought forth: with the very blood of your heart. (Beauty) will rise from your heart to your song, having purified you first" (*Desolation*, p. 207). This process of purification and liberation is effected in the "Nocturne," transmuting the acrimony into fatigue, the rebellious imprecation into trusting prayer, and clothing these feelings in beautiful, precise, moving language. In the poems that follow, in the section "Nature" (*Naturaleza*), the passion, purified by artistic catharsis, is freed from exaggerated sensuality. It flows into purer verse, more objective lyricism, still intense but as if diffused in fog, mist, in the desolate snows of the Antarctic. In Gabriela Mistral's poetry—as in that of all the fine poets of the Spanish language—realism is gradually transformed into idealism, and sensual pleasure into ascetism, into *memento mori*.

Puerto Rico

THE POETIC theme of Puerto Rico, its people and landscape may be considered as one aspect of the great theme of America, so prominent in the poetry of Gabriela Mistral. In her first book, *Desolation* (1922), there are no allusions to Puerto Rico; neither are there any in *Tenderness*—we are acquainted only with the revised edition of 1945—nor in *Wine Press* (1954), her last publication, although all of these books touch on the American theme. *Desolation* contains the round "Let us Sing on Chilean Soil" (*Cantemos en Tierra Chilena*), and in the section "Nature" (*Naturaleza*) there are several descriptive poems of Patagonia; these are completely subjective visions, lonely frozen stretches of snow and wind that reflect the poet's own intimate desolation. In *Tenderness* the American themes are the basis for stories, rounds, and lullabies, some of them reproduced from former books, others of more recent composition. In *Wine Press*, she elaborates upon the theme, with tone and shadings closer to the style of the two "Hymns" (*Himnos*) in *Felling*. *Felling*, published in 1938, is only a partial compilation of the vast poetic production of sixteen years. It was written after Gabriela's visits to Puerto Rico, when she came to know its people, landscape, and way of being. It is not strange that Puerto Rico was then incorporated into her poetic world.

The poems of American theme in *Felling* are generally more objective in style than those of *Desolation;* in addition, they have deliberate intents that go beyond the aesthetic end. Not only do they form the entire section "America" but they are also scattered here and there throughout the other sections of the book. Among the latter, we find those that were completely inspired by Puerto Rican themes: "Caribbean Sea" (*Mar Caribe*) and "Message for the Antilles" (*Recado para las Antillas*); there are also brief references to Puerto Rico—some direct, some indirect—in "Salt" (*Sal*), "Water" (*Agua*), "Cascade in Barren Soil" (*Cascada en sequedal*), "Mountain Range" (*Cordillera*), "Land of Absence" (*País de la ausencia*), and "Drink" (*Beber*).

The presence of the Puerto Rican themes in this work cannot be explained solely by Gabriela's then recent visits to that country and her friendship with its people. There is in Gabriela a constant preoccupation with America, a Pan-Hispanic Americanism that springs from her direct contact with the soil in the years of her rural childhood, from her unsatisfied maternal longings projected upon these landscapes and towns over which she watches as a mother protects her children. Some of her political and pedagogical aims and the will to affirm that which is Hispanic-American in contrast to that which is of Spain, Europe, or the United States, although for different reasons in each case, confirm and intensify this preoccupation. Gabriela does not forget that Puerto Rico is a part of that Hispanic America that she loves, bound to it by ties of blood, language, and culture. It is as important to her as are Mexico or Chile. Above all, it is important to her that Puerto Rico regain consciousness of her relationship with those peoples, and that she affirm it of her own free will. She is seduced by its pleasant climate and the gentle character of its inhabitants; she is disturbed by its precarious political situation and its uncertain future. Perhaps, for reasons of health, she preferred the sunny lands of the tropics, and for reasons of temperament, the people of friendly, quiet, gentle manner, little inclined to polemic and contradiction. In Puerto Rico and with Puerto Ricans she always claimed to feel very much at home. This does not mean that she thought the island a perfect paradise, or its people angels. She saw with perfect clarity the national and individual defects and used to become angry and remonstrate with us about them. On occasion she intervened on behalf of the country or of some distinguished Puerto Rican when she felt that it was a question of truth, justice, or ethics. She never denied her attention and help whenever they were requested of her.

Her interest in the island was manifested not only in her verses but in the numerous prose articles published for a decade in the journal *Puerto Rico Illustrated* (*Puerto Rico Ilustrado*) or in those Hispanic-American dailies that she favored with her assiduous collaboration: *El Mercurio* of Chile, *La Nación* of Buenos Aires, *El Tiempo* of Bogotá, *El Universal* of Caracas. One could compile a thick tome of these prose writings that praise Puerto Rico and its people in an impassioned, almost folkloric, deliberately disordered language. A study of those materials would produce the evidence of her love, of her eager desire to understand and encourage the country. She wanted to make it known to the other lands that shared its language and culture. To a large degree she achieved this.

But let us return to the poems of Puerto Rican inspiration, to those of *Felling*. In the first one, "Salt" (*Sal*), (pp. 78–80), we find a general allusion, brief and not too precise:

> Mano a mano nos tenemos,
> como Raquel, como Rebeca.
> Yo volteo su cuerpo roto
> y ella voltea mi quedeja,
> y nos contamos las Antillas
> o desvariamos las Provenzas.
>
> lines 31–36.

> Hand in hand we clasp each other
> Like Rachel and Rebecca.
> I turn her broken body
> And she turns my tresses,
> And we tell each other of the Antilles
> Or wildly dream about Provence.

It is a meeting and almost mystic communion of the poet with humble, common, familiar subject matter. The intimate dialogue is begun: they speak of the known and the beloved lands. The line "and we tell each other of the Antilles" already contains the childhood vision of the islands that she will repeat afterwards in other poems; islands of which stories can be "told" because imagination and sentiment have clothed them in fable and marvel.

In "Water" (*Agua*), the allusion is equally brief, but more specific, more concrete:

> *Hay países que yo recuerdo*
> *como recuerdo mis infancias.*
> *Son países de mar o río,*
> *de pastales, de vegas y aguas,*
> *Aldea mía sobre el Ródano,*
> *rendida en río y en cigarras;*
> *Antilla en palmas verdi-negras*
> *que a medio mar está y me llama;*
> *¡roca lígure de Portofino,*
> *mar italiana, mar italiana!*
>   p. 81, lines 1–10.

> There are lands that I remember
> As I remember childhood days.
> They are lands of sea or river,
> Of pastures, lowlands, waterways.
> Village of mine upon the Rhone,
> Surrendered to river and cicadas;
> Antilla in green-black palms
> Calling me in the midst of the sea;
> Ligurian rock of Portofino,
> Italian sea, Italian sea!

The evocation of Antilla is a tender one, as in dreams. The use of the singular gives us strong reasons to suspect that the reference was only to Puerto Rico. (Cuba does not appear as a poetic theme until *Wine Press*; Santo Domingo is always absent.) It is a landscape of humid, undulating, peaceful lands, of grazing fields, lowlands, and waters, as if taken from one of Garcilaso's pastoral poems. The singular theme of the "green-black palms" is noted with its exact shade of color. The island is in the midst of the sea. Viewed from such a distance, from her own nostalgia, the poet mentally contrasts the smallness of the island with the vastness of the ocean; that "it calls to me" reveals to us the bond of love, the attraction it exercises over her watchful heart. The two nine-syllable lines contain the seed of the poetic vision of "Caribbean Sea" (*Mar Caribe*), the most beautiful of the poems dedicated to Puerto Rico.

Incidentally, and as if surprised at the irrationality of her own happiness, she again alludes to that land in the first stanza of "Cascade in Barren Soil" (*Cascada en sequedal*):

Ganas tengo de cantar	I have a desire to sing
sin razón de mi algarada:	Without any reason for my
ni vivo en la tierra	joy:
de donde es la palma.	Nor am I even of the land
p. 83, lines 1–4.	Where the palm tree dwells.

Again, there is the palm, a constant, determinate theme of the Mistralian view of the Puerto Rican landscape. Living in that land would be enough to set the fountain of joy and song flowing. There is no higher praise for its spirituality and beauty.

The desire that Puerto Rico be incorporated into the community of Hispanic-American peoples is formulated in "Hymn to the Mountain Range" (*Himno a la cordillera*) (pp. 98–104).

> *Al fueguino sube el Caribe*
> *por tus punas espejeadas;*
> *a criaturas de salares*
> *y de pinar, lleva a las palmas.*
> stanza 12, lines 1–4.

> To Tierra del Fuego the Caribbean flows
> Through your shining table lands
> Creatures of salt and pinegrove,
> Are carried to where the palm trees grow.

Let us take note that "the palm trees" are the Antilles, Puerto Rico; so great an importance does the poet give to this species of its flora! So strongly is she impressed by the palms as a distinctive trait of the island landscape!

In the strange poem "Land of Absence" (*País de la ausencia*) (pp. 125–27), she describes that land of mist and shadows that she has forged for herself with the nostalgias of her long exile in Europe:

Me nació de cosas	It was born to me of things
que no son país:	That are not country:
de patrias y patrias	Of the many lands
que tuve y perdí;	I had and could not keep;
de las criaturas	Of the children
que yo vi morir;	Whose death I did see;
de lo que era mío	Of what once was mine
y se fué de mí.	And has gone from me.

Perdí cordilleras	I lost mountain ranges
en donde dormí;	Where I once did sleep;
perdí huertos de oro	I lost golden orchards
dulces de vivir,	With living sweet;
perdí yo las islas	I lost the islands
de caña y añil,	Of cane and azure deep
y las sombras de ellos	And as their shadows merged
me las vi ceñir	I could see
y juntas y amantes	Them together and loving
hacerse país.	Make a land for me.
lines 29–46.	

Among the lost and recovered things in the imaginary land, she counts the islands of cane and indigo, the sugar cane field and the intense blue of the sky, elements that should be included with those mentioned before. The poet speaks of these islands as if they were her own lands, the memory of which nourishes and sustains her in her exile. Her love holds them in as great esteem as her native land; they appear here joined to the evocation of the Andes and of the Central Valley of Chile.

Another poem, "Drink" (*Beber*) (pp. 129–131), also springs from the feeling of nostalgia; it imaginatively reproduces four analogous scenes that have occurred in different times and places.

> *Recuerdo gestos de criaturas*
> *y eran gestos de darme agua.*
> lines 1–2.

> I remember gestures of little children
> And they were gestures of giving me water.

One of the scenes unfolds in Puerto Rico, near the sea, at siesta time (seen *En la Isla de Puerto Rico* . . . on p. 14 of this book). The poet places before the reader the omnipresent, intense blue of the tropical afternoon, the graceful disorder of the waves, the drowsy sway of innumerable palm trees. Their fresh shade over her prone body, their boughs pendulous with fruit, the warm sweetness of the coconut milk suggest to her the image of mother's milk, of the hundred mothers who lull her to sleep and nurse her like a child, that offer her a sweetness never before felt. In "Caribbean Sea" (*Mar Caribe*) the image is repeated, but with reference to the stars of the nocturnal sky:

| *de sus constelaciones* | by its constellations |
| *amamantada.* | nursed. |

That maternal sweetness of the coconut milk and of the starry night, of the soft whisper of the foliage, are like symbols of the tenderness of Puerto Rico, of the gentle character of its inhabitants: a moral retreat in which the poet knew peace and happiness and perhaps remembered the caresses of her mother, so recently dead. The other scenes take place in Chile and Mexico; in Gabriela's heart, Puerto Rico had the same place as the American lands she loved most.

The landscape of the island and interior of a Puerto Rican house serve as the setting for "Message for the Antilles" (*Recado para las Antillas*), the almost story-like life of a twenty-year old girl, a reader of poetry. Gabriela had said of these "Messages" that they were written in a tone that was most characteristically hers, that peculiar rural inflection with which she had lived and with which she would die. There is no rural tone in the poem we are dealing with now, but there is a happy, sustained note of pleasure and admiration. The intense poetic quality, the beauty and exactness of the images, lend to the description of the island's exterior and the domestic interior as a luminous, light grace not too frequent in Gabriela's verses.

> *La Isla celebra fiesta de la niña.*
> *el Trópico es como Dios absoluto*
> *y en esos soles se muere o se salva.*
> *Anda el café como un alma vehemente;*
> *en venas anda de valle o montaña*
> *y punza el sueño de niños oscuros;*
> *hierve en el pan y sosiega en el agua.*
>
> *De leño tiene su casa la niña*
> *y llega el viento del mar a su cama;*
> *abre en truhán con olor de plantíos*
> *y entran en él toronjales y cañas.*
>
> . . . .
> *La negra sirve un café subterráneo,*
> *denso en el vértigo y casto en la nata.*
> *Entra partida de su delantal,*
> *de risa grande y bandeja de plata.*
>
> *Yo, que no estoy, se la mando a que llegue*
> *tosca y divina como es una fábula,*

y mientras bebe la niña su néctar
la negra dice su ensalmo de magia.

. . . .

Los mozos llegan a la hora de siesta;
son del color de la piña y el ámbar.
Cuando la miran la mientan su sangre
si consintiese, lamaránla Patria.

En medio de ellos parece la piña,
entre su mata ceñida de espadas.
En medio de ellos es el flamboyant,
llama que el viento tajea en mil llamas.

. . . .

Ahora duerme en cardumen de oro
del cielo tórrido, junto a las palmas,
adormecida en su Isla de fuego,
pura en su tierra y en su agua antillana.

Duerme su noche de aromas y duerme
sus mocedades que aun son infancias.
¡Duerme su patria que son tres Antillas
y los destinos que están en su raza!

The Island honors the young girl's fiesta.
The Tropics are like an absolute God
And in those suns one dies or lives.
The coffee hovers like a vivid soul;
It flows through veins of valley or mountain
And punctures the sleep of dark children;
Simmers in bread and rests in water.

The house of the young girl is of wood
And the sea breeze touches her bed;
Knavishly steals in with the fragrance of plantings
Bringing with it grapefruit and cane.

. . . .

The negress serves a darkened coffee,
Swirlingly thick and pure in its cream.
She enters with body cleft by apron,
With a broad laugh and silver tray.

I, who am not there, call her to come
Coarse and divine she is, like a fable,
And while the young girl drinks her nectar
The negress chants her magic spell.

. . . .

The boys arrive at siesta time;
They are the color of pineapple and amber.

When they gaze at her they call forth her blood
If she agreed, they would call her Nation.

In their midst appears the pineapple,
Within its body girded by swords.
In their midst the flamboyan,
Flame that the wind multiplies in thousands.

. . . .

Now she sleeps on a golden shoal
Of torrid sky, next to the palms,
Asleep on her island of fire,
Pure of soil and of Antillian sea.

Asleep her night of fragrance and
Asleep her youth like childhood days.
Asleep her country of three Antilles
And the destinies that are in her race!

The vision here is broader and more detailed. New motifs are added to the already familiar ones of palm trees, blue sky, and sugar cane field: golden sparkles of sunlight, fragrances of garden plantings and grapefruit orchards, the pineapple with its girdle of swords, the blaze of the "flamboyan tree," the intense night perfume. The halo of magic also envelops the figures: the negress with the hearty laugh and the broad apron, the girls who flutter about like brown-spotted doves, the young men the color of pineapple and amber who come at siesta time. Everything has the air of a fable about it, and there is a vague analogy to the story of the Sleeping Beauty of the Forest; everything makes one think that Gabriela attributes to Puerto Rico a quality of fable, of natural poetry.

In "Caribbean Sea" this attribution is deliberate. The title places the island in its exact geographic position. As in "Water" (*Agua*), she emphasizes its helplessness on the immensity of the sea. The date of the composition is given at the bottom of the poem: "On the day of the liberation of the Philippines." It is obvious that the poem was born of a political sentiment, of the need to repair an injustice. Puerto Rico and the Philippine Islands, North American colonies, the last spoils of the Spanish empire, should, in the poet's opinion, share similar destinies. It was not so, and the good fortune of the Philippines is contrasted with the misfortune of Puerto Rico. The poet urges that justice be distributed equitably:

Isla de Puerto Rico	Island of Puerto Rico,
isla de palmas,	Island of palms,
apenas cuerpo, apenas,	Barely a body,
como la Santa,	Barely like the Saint,
apenas posadura	Barely perched upon the
sobre las aguas.	waters.
La que como María	She who like María
funde al nombrarla	Vanishes at the naming
y que, como paloma,	And that like a dove
vuela, nombrada;	Flies, once named!
del millar de palmeras	Of the thousand palms the
como más alta,	highest,
y en las dos mil colinas	And on the two thousand hills
como llamada.	as if summoned.
Isla en amanaceres	Island of dawns
de mí gozada	enjoyed by me
sin cuerpo acongojada,	Without pained body,
trémula de alma;	Tremulous of soul;
de sus constelaciones	By its constellations
amamantada,	nursed,
en la siesta de fuego	And in the fiery siesta
punzada de hablas,	Pierced by murmurs,
y otra vez en el alba	And again in the dawn
adoncellada.	A maiden once more.
Isla en caña y cafés	Island in cane and coffees
apasionada . . .	Passionate . . .
. . . .	*. . . . .*
Te salven los Arcángeles	May the Archangels of
de nuestra raza:	Our race save you:
Miguel castigador,	Michael chastiser,
Rafael que marcha,	Raphael who walks,
y Gabriel que conduce	And Gabriel who signals
la hora colmada.	The brimming hour.
Antes que en mí se acaben	Before there cease in me
marcha y mirada;	Movement and sight;
antes que carne mía	Before this flesh of mine
ya sea fábula;	Becomes a fable;
antes que mis rodillas	Before my knees
vuelen en ráfagas.	Tremble like gusts of wind.

The six stanzas of "Caribbean Sea" are grouped into two symmetric units of different length. The three initial ones—about thirty-six lines—sing the praises of Puerto Rico; the three final ones—twenty lines—formulate the prayer for the salvation of the island. The entire poem is written in the *seguidilla* rhythm: alternate lines of seven and five syllables, with assonantal rhyme in the even lines. Within the uniform meter of this movement, some variants underline the poetic intent. The first part advances with slow regularity, highlighting the beautiful procession of images. As one approaches the third stanza, the alternation of sharp and brief endings quickens the rhythm, lending it tension and warmth; then, for a moment, it is suspended in the broad, pathetic, final phrase—"Cordelia of the waves, bitter Cordelia"—only to be hurled immediately into the swiftness of the second part. Here the vehemence of the prayer gives the words a shortened, rapid movement that draws back sharply with the foreboding of death in the two final words of the last lines, with their antepenultimate accents: two shudders, like gusts of wind. The syntactic parallelism of the phrases—series of epithets, comparisons, wishes, expressions of time—reinforces the rhythmic monotony; but, at the same time, it intensifies the admiring, impassioned tone. There is a repetition of the fervor and insistence of the Marian litanies, to which it comes closest in language. It is a litany that sings of the uniqueness of the island, as a charming, graceful creature. In Gabriela Mistral's poetry there are several moments like this one, in which an object is suddenly revealed to her in all of its marvelous beauty, an experience that overwhelms the poet with mystical rapture.

The landscape in this poem is described in terms of three or four essential details: tall, slender palms, two thousand hills, small territorial size. Like a bird with more voice than flesh, the island seems to perch for a moment on the waters just before taking flight.

apenas cuerpo, apenas	Barely a body, barely
como la Santa,	Like the Saint,
apenas posadura	Barely perched
sobre las aguas.	Upon the waters.

The triple repetition of "barely" (*apenas*) heightens that note of spirituality; the palms, the hills withdraw from the physical and earthly realm. The comparison with the Virgin Mary prepares us for the symbol of the perennial virginity of Puerto Rico.

In the second stanza the island is transformed into a maiden, almost a child. But for a brief instant the pure images give way to erotic ones. The poet has rejoiced in this beauty with the tremulous, ardent pleasure of possession. The diurnal cycle is captured in three moments: at dawn, the constellations—mothers who nurse the island-child with the milk of stars. They bathe her in their serene light of centuries. At noon, the heat, the thousand noises of the tropics offend her virginal purity; but at dawn her virginity is again restored. It is a beautiful, skillful contrast between the motherly night, the voluptuous siesta, and the clean, innocent clarity of the Puerto Rican dawn.

In the third stanza the note of praise is heightened. The island again becomes passionate, "sweet to speak of, blessed in song." Those extremes are fused into a balance: "island passionate in cane and coffees." It is compared to a child, to a religious hymn of triumph. Its tenderness, its innocence evoke tragic symbols in the poet—"Siren without song," "bitter Cordelia," "Iphigenia alive in the flame." These immediately precede the prayer, the vehement wishes expressed in the second part. We pass from the objective vision of the essential elements of the landscape to the subjective vision that transforms the object in terms of the ideal. Very beautiful, profound religious and literary myths are used to explain the uniqueness and misfortune of this marvelous being.

At the beginning of the fourth stanza—which initiates the second part—she prays for the salvation of Puerto Rico. Like all things of extraordinary value, it must be redeemed. The third stanza expresses her wish that the archangels be the saviors; the final one prays that the act be fulfilled before the poet's death. Gabriela died without seeing her wish fulfilled.

There is in this poem more than a mere civic preoccupation, more than an obligation to do political justice. The poet sees clearly that the role of colony impairs the spirit. She perceives the moral disorder and is upset by it; she is aware of the danger that deprivation of liberty and the clash with an antagonistic culture represent for an authentic culture. The "may you be saved," and "may the archangels of our race save you" express the measure of that danger and the profound and transcendental value that freedom has for the poet. One also notes in these phrases the depth of her anguish as she contemplates the reality and perceives all of its possible consequences. To save signifies, as in the religious sense of the word, to achieve the plenitude and perfection of one's own being, to purify oneself, to perpetuate oneself in the contemplation of God: the spiritual summit, happiness.

Thus, she commends the salvation of the island to the three archangels of "our race": Michael, the vanquisher of the devil; Raphael, God's healer; Gabriel, harbinger of good news: Salvation is to be attained through mediators who belong to the Hispanic cultural community; in other words, through the redeeming, liberating abilities inherent in our own values. Nor does Gabriela entrust this salvation to limited individual effort, because this is a matter of redemption of a select being, marked by grace: "white roe deer," "new llama of Pachacámac," "golden egg of the brood," "Iphigenia, alive in the flame." Does the poet perhaps fear to entrust the precious and difficult task to inadequate human effort? Her song rises like a prayer pleading for a miracle. And her love sets the time limit because she wishes to witness the redemption and share in its joy. The time limit is her own life:

antes de que en mí se acaben	Before there cease in me
marcha y mirada;	Movement and sight;
antes que carne mía	Before this flesh of mine
ya sea fábula;	Becomes a fable;
antes que mis rodillas	Before my knees
vuelen en ráfagas.	Tremble like gusts of wind.

Relations with the United States

DIRECT CONTACT

Gabriela Mistral's relations with the United States began in 1922 with the publication of *Desolation* by the Hispanic Institute and continued until her death in 1957. Frequent visits to the country, long sojourns at eastern colleges and universities where she analyzed Hispanic-American literature and culture, her friendship with illustrious North Americans—Waldo Frank, Charles and Anne Lindbergh, Leo Rowe, Erna Fergusson, Margaret Bates—strengthened the friendly admiration she had always had for the North American nation.

In February 1922, as stated earlier, Dr. Federico de Onís, a professor at Columbia University, lectured on Gabriela's poetic work before a group of North American professors of Spanish. His audience was deeply impressed by the poetry and personality of the great Chilean poetess and teacher. They listened to a harsh, ardent voice and discovered an American woman of extraordinary qualities and spirit. When they realized that those poems were still scattered through journals and newspapers, they conceived the generous and far-sighted idea of gathering them together in a book to be published at their expense. Thus it came about that, with the author's consent, the first edition of *Desolation* was published in the United States. This was the first and strongest bond with which destiny united Gabriela and the United States.

Two years later, in 1924, moved by the desire to get to know the country, Gabriela came to New York on her way to Spain, accompanied by her intimate friend, the well-known Mexican professor, Palma Guillén. With her, Gabriela visited the places of historic and artistic interest and met Dr. Onís, to whom she expressed her gratitude for the publication of her work.

In 1930 Barnard College of Columbia University invited her to give a course in Hispanic-American literature. She spent the fall and spring semesters there; in February 1931 she received a similar invitation from Vassar College, where she remained until June. I remember having heard her say how she enjoyed being with the students and discussing everything under the sun with them. She admired the girls' youthful energy, their ease of manner, their independent character, frankness, and great curiosity about everything. Through these conversations she came to know at firsthand the spirit of the North American people.

In the summer of that same year she filled the chair of Hispanic-American literature in the School of Languages of Middlebury College in Vermont. The idyllic beauty of the Green Mountains, on the shores of Lake Dunmore, the splen did elms and maples in Hepburn Hall park, the intimate, almost home-like atmosphere of the Spanish school captivated her. She always remembered with nostalgia the months spent in that delightful retreat and the welcoming, friendly, if somewhat reserved, manner of the people of New England.

In 1938 she travelled to the United States for the third time. From Cuba she came to Miami and took up residence in historic Saint Augustine, where she remained for two months From there she visited some southern cities—Jacksonville, Tallahassee, Mobile, New Orleans, where she lingered to attend the Mardi Gras celebration. During her stop in Georgia, on the way to New York, she attempted to visit her friend Dr. Pedro Albizu Campos, who was being held in the federal prison at Atlanta for political reasons. She was not granted permission to see him and so continued on to Washington. There, as a guest of the Pan American Union, she lectured on the human geography of Chile. She made several friends in Washington: Dr. Leo Rowe, Concha Romero James, Francisco Aguilera. Upon her appointment as Chilean Consul in Nice, she sailed for France from the port of New York.

She did not return to the United States until 1946, after having received the Nobel Prize for Literature. Her country had just appointed her Consul in Los Angeles. The Union of American Women availed itself of her stay in Washington to confer upon her the title of "Woman of the Americas." Immediately afterwards she crossed the continent to assume her new responsibilities.

For a year she lived in Monrovia, near Pasadena; but she was not entirely happy with the climate and moved to Santa Barbara, where she bought a lovely large house surrounded by gardens and an orchard.

During this period she was ill and depressed. Nevertheless, she continued to receive visits from her North and South American friends, writers, professors, and artists: Marta Salotti, Eda Ramelli, Erna Fergusson, Raúl Haya de la Torre, Arturo Torres Rioseco, Ciro Alegría, María Luisa Bombal, Pedro Manuel González. Her friendship with Doris Dana, with whom she lived during the last years of her life, whom she named executrix of her will, and to whom she entrusted her work and unpublished manuscripts, dates from this time.

Many of the poems of *Wine Press*, her last work, were written in Santa Barbara. The inhabitants of this city offered a testimonial dinner at the Hotel Mar Monte, both to Gabriela and Robert Millikan, also a Nobel Prize winner. In her acceptance speech, Gabriela paid tribute to the Scandinavian people for their cultural contributions and their constant efforts in behalf of world peace. She spoke in Spanish and Professor Eda Ramelli of the University of California translated her words into English.

When the University of California at Los Angeles and Mills College in Oakland awarded her honorary doctoral degrees, she went personally to accept them and availed herself of the trip to visit Berkeley, Oakland, San Diego, Long Beach, Pasadena, and Ojai, where she was disappointed in her hopes to see Krishnamurti.

For reasons of health she left for Mexico and lived for a long time in the state of Veracruz; the condition of her heart did not permit her to live up on the high plateau. When she passed through New Orleans, the mayor symbolically presented her with the keys of the city and honored her with a trip along the great Mississippi River.

She returned to Europe as the Chilean Consul in Naples. When she again came to New York, it was to settle for good on Long Island, in Doris Dana's home at 15 Spruce Street, Roslyn Harbor. At Columbia University's Bicentennial in 1954, she was awarded an honorary doctoral degree. As long as her physical energies permitted, she received visitors, wrote, and attended important public functions.

Toward the end of 1956 she entered Hempstead General Hospital, where she died on January 10, 1957. The news of her death brought to the funeral home not only her intimate friends, but also many Spanish-Americans residing in the city, representatives of the diplomatic and consular Corps, writers, and artists. In St. Patrick's Cathedral, with the Chilean priest Rev. Renato Poblete of Fordham officiating, there were solemn funeral honors for her eternal peace and a mass was sung for the body lying in state. The United States Government offered Chile an official airplane for removal of the body to Santiago. The North American professors who had published *Desolation* in 1922 had not then suspected that the great Chilean poetess' destiny, her glory, and her death would be so closely linked to the United States.

THE UNITED STATES AS A LITERARY THEME

The United States as a theme appeared for the first time in Gabriela Mistral's literary work in the year 1922. On September 18 of that year, she published the article "Mexico and the United States," in the *Repertorio Americano* of San José, Costa Rica. From that date until 1948, the United States was a repeated theme in about thirty articles, which appeared in *El Mercurio* of Chile, *La Nueva Democracia*, *El Repertorio Americano*, *Puerto Rico Ilustrado*, and the *Boletín* of the Pan American Union. She may have written many more; however, the difficulty of locating these prose works written for the daily press of so many different countries has made it impossible to examine them.

Those I have been able to read deal with the following themes: true Pan-Americanism and the relations between the United States and Spanish America; the death of Sandino; agreements and differences among the Americas; eulogies of North American artists and writers like Waldo Frank, Isidora Duncan, Alice Stone Blackwell, Dr. Leo Rowe, Mrs. Frances Horne; the transatlantic flight of Charles A. Lindbergh and his visit to South America; the moral and practical virtues of the North American people; their militant Christianity and their social sense; Catholicism in the United States; the interest in Hispanic culture and studies manifested in intellectual centers and universities throughout the country.

As one considers this list of themes one notes that what concerned Gabriela above all else were the relations between the North American people and the peoples to the south of the Rio Grande: the political as well as the cultural relations. She knew that only mutual friendship and good will could give those relationships positive and creative meaning. Very conscious of her personal responsibility, she approached the North American people with a true desire to understand them, without prejudices of any kind, moved by a spirit of justice and fairness. She loved the peace and harmony of the towns. With her deeply rooted Spanish sense of universalism, she wanted to achieve an understanding and cooperation that would rise above all narrow nationalisms and regionalisms. As a Hispano-American, she deeply regretted what seemed to her the errors of official North American policy in its relations with the peoples to the south; she was hurt by the economic exploitation, by the armed interventions, by the moral and material support of dictators, by the almost complete ignorance of Hispanic spirit, culture, customs, and idiosyncracies. But this critical view never caused hate or resentment on her part. She adopted, on the contrary, a free and creative attitude of love, with faith in men and nations and with firm confidence in the final triumph of reason, truth, and goodness. She frankly admired the virtues she observed in the North Americans and hoped that some day, if both Americas were willing to lay aside their mutual suspicions and resentments and rectify the errors of the past, the true brotherhood she desired would finally be realized.

She tried to work toward this ideal of brotherhood, justice, and mutual respect through her articles. Her attitude can be compared to the attitude of the Cuban José Martí toward the United States: a noble and exacting effort, a critical consciousness of reality, a faith in the ability of men and nations to overcome their errors and weaknesses through the noble and selfless action of the spirit. She never doubted that this ideal could be realized; but she knew that it would take effort, pain, sacrifice, and that it would demand slow and very patient work.

In her first article, "Mexico and the United States," dedicated to the North American students who were attending the summer school at the National University of Mexico, she spoke of the necessary friendship of those two countries. After praising Mexico very warmly, she urged the students to get to know it and to love it, and she begged them to make Mexico known to their countrymen when they returned to their own land. Mexico "is the arm that Spanish America extends toward the United States in a desire for justice and understanding. This arm will take back to those in the South either a gesture of friendship, or of suspicion." She asked of these students understanding and justice for South America and urged them to lend their good will and efforts to the work of building continental peace. She found in the gesture of the North American teachers who paid for the publication of her book an example of what love and unselfishness could achieve: "My first book is at this very moment being printed in the presses of New York and it will be presented to me as a material and spiritual gift by the teachers who understood the soul of their sister without having seen her face."

She noted the same exemplary feeling in the conduct of Waldo Frank, Leo S. Rowe, and Mrs. Horne, to name but a few of her many North American friends. She admired the beauty of Mrs. Horne's paintings of flowers, work she considered very feminine: and above all she praised her for having dedicated her fine and detailed art to the loving, careful representation of the Puerto Rican flora. While living in Puerto Rico, Mrs. Horne did not remain a stranger to her surroundings; she spent her leisure hours in getting to know the country, and with her exact and beautiful drawings she contributed to the scientific knowledge of its native plant life.

Dr. Leo S. Rowe, another of Gabriela's friends, was director of the Pan American Union. Gabriela recalled his prolonged sojourn in Chile and in other South American countries, his understanding and appreciation of its men, its culture, its problems, and the special services he always performed for them with the greatest pleasure. He always had faith in peace between the nations and he dedicated his life to the ideal of establishing friendly and just relations among all the American peoples.

Conversely, when in February 1939 Dr. Rowe introduced Gabriela Mistral at the Pan American Union, he pointed out that "she has dreamed of our nations united, loving each other, teaching each other and mutually protecting each other and has set an example of what true Pan American friendship and cooperation are."

She spoke of Waldo Frank as of a brother. On one occasion, as she was giving her compatriot Professor Arturo Torres Rioseco an affectionate embrace, she assured him that he and Waldo Frank were the only men to whom she had ever shown her affection in this particular way. Frank was for her "a rare Yankee, a mystic as well as an earth dweller, one who loves the earth as a pedestal to the Divine." She deeply appreciated his "quiet work of twenty years, his eager effort to explain the South to the North, his having worked in behalf of Spanish-Americans without being expressly asked, without reservations, and without pay." Frank's attitude toward the peoples of the South seemed perfect to her. "For us," she said, "you learned Spanish and you penetrated the forest of the language and reached its most elusive corners." This broad, intimate knowledge of Spanish had enabled Frank "to perceive our essence beneath the crust."

We should state in passing that Gabriela considered it indispensable to know the language of a people if one were truly to know and understand them. In 1937, in the pages of the *Revista Hispánica Moderna*, she advised students of Spanish in the United States to learn that language not for business or political reasons but out of love for it and for the culture it represented and as a means of spiritual rapprochement with Latin America. At the same time, in a letter to Alberto Rembao in 1940, she spoke of her own efforts to attain some command of English and she lamented having learned it so late. When she compared it to Spanish, she praised its more rapid rhythm and its sense of the concrete, and she stated that she was attempting to capture and make use of those "virtues." This confession indicates to what extent she was interested in English and had undertaken its study.

But let us return to her friendship with Waldo Frank. She considered this North American writer one of the few truly free men of the contemporary world. Distressed by the extent to which totalitarian ideologies had spread in modern times, she warned him to take care because "heads are being hunted now as they were never before hunted in the ancient struggle between men and beasts. A high price has been set on about a hundred free heads that still walk this earth unafraid and unguarded, but marked by the markers," by those who are searching "for the few hearts who are shouting the alert to those who sleep." "You, builder," she told him, "watch yourself for America." I should note that Gabriela rarely went too far in her praise of people because she was very demanding of herself and of others. The fervor, the tenderness with which she spoke of Waldo Frank on several occasions, are indicative of the gratitude, the friendship, and the esteem that she felt for this illustrious and generous North American.

When Gabriela died, on January 10, 1957, Waldo Frank wrote a brief, intense, and lucid eulogy of her character and work. As we read it, we cannot help but admire this Northern writer's extraordinary ability to penetrate and interpret the soul and language of a woman of South America, and we realize that such an ability can only be attained through a work of love, through the living, creative generosity of a free and just spirit.

Gabriela Mistral's efforts to promote peace and cooperation among all the American nations was founded on her belief in the existence of a continental unity, of a spirit and destiny common to all the peoples of this hemisphere. In the "Message," written on April 14, 1931, on the occasion of the first Pan American Day, she expounded her view as to what constitutes that

American unity. She considered one of the most important factors to be the "liberality and generosity of America, that of her geographic breadth, in calling men from the four corners of the earth to create universal races, capable of broadening the classic life and capable of all future epics." A second factor of considerable importance is the "assurance of American body and conscience as it faces the great undertaking, and confidence in the future." She affirmed that all the American nations love peace and conceive of war as a thing of the past, definitely behind us.

"Our peoples also have in common the fact that they have been nursed by the milk of twenty-two constitutions that proclaim respect for another's independence as a primary condition of personal integrity. Given life by Washington and Bolívar beneath the guiding light of international law, they are obliged to serve the independence of other lands with the same dignity as their own."

In the very heart of their civil conscience, Gabriela believed, they reject injustice and violence in international relations because they consider them a detraction from their own honor and glory. Although she realized that on several occasions some of the American nations had unfortunately strayed from these truly ideal moral standards, she was confident that they would rectify their errors, overcome their suspicions and resentments, and attain that happy future of harmony, justice, and union, to which they aspire.

Few statesmen, few politicians have worked as assiduously as Gabriela toward this beautiful goal. She was moved by a profound and authentic Christian spirit based on justice and love. She considered herself *American* in the broadest sense of the word; both the grandeur and misery of America were her innermost concerns. Her maternal inclinations sought to protect all the American countries as children of her spirit, and she watched over them with the prophetic and selfless view of a poet and of the most tender and far-seeing mother.

In Gabriela's first books of verses, *Desolation*, *Tenderness*, and *Felling*, there was not a single poem that dealt with the United

States as a motif of poetic inspiration. In *Wine Press*, 1954, her last work, the theme appeared probably as a consequence of her sojourn in Santa Barbara, from 1946 on. This fact throws light upon her process of poetic creation. Gabriela was never moved to literary creation by abstract thought, mere reflection, or pure ideas or feelings. All of her poems were born of an immediate and physical contact with reality, of her concrete and direct relationship to something, whether it was a person, a landscape, or an object. The beings of nature, children, men, and their actions were the sources of her song. When the human and natural landscapes of the North American West became the focal point of her gaze and attention, they stimulated her imagination and moved her to write the poems "California Poppy" (*Amapola de California*), "Little Okote Pine" (*Ocotillo*), and "Birth of a House" (*Nacimiento de una casa*).

The first of these poems is a song to the poppy of California, a small marvel of warmth and praise. The poet personifies the flower, giving it a soul; she identifies with it and reveals the common destiny that binds them.

¡Pobre gloria tuya y mía	Sad glory yours and mine
(pobre tu alma, pobre mi	(Sad your soul, sad my soul)
alma)	To burn of our own accord
arder sin atizadura	And as if impaled,
e igual que acicateadas,	On some far shore of the
en una orilla del mundo,	world
caídas de nuestra Llama!	Fallen from our Llama!

Both are children of the spirit, both burn with passion, both find themselves almost exiles in this place. The poet is lost in enchanted contemplation of this small and ardent being, "the color of flowing honey," ephemeral, without any other apparent value but that of being testimony to the creative work of God and of giving thanks to him.

En la palma apenas duras	In my palms you hardly last
y recoges, de tomada,	And once plucked, you
como unos labios sorbidos	withdraw
tus cuatro palabras rápidas	Your four words rapidly
cuando te rompen lo erguido	Like tasted lips,
y denso de la alabanza.	When they break your lofty
lines 13–18.	Fullbodied beauty.

The religious sense of the poem is clear. The poppy reveals the mystery of its being and of its ultimate end. Like the Spanish Mystic Fray Luis de Granada, Gabriela discovers the incalculable value of things that have no apparent use: they have been created as a gratuitous gift of God, as evidence of his glory, and to delight the senses of men with their beauty.

When she crossed the Arizona desert on her way to Mexico, she must have remembered her Chilean desert of Atacama, of which she had written in the delightful article "Small Audible Map of Chile" (*Pequeño Mapa Audible de Chile*). What her faithful memory retained of this desert was the monotonous and harsh noise of the mechanical drill breaking up the minerals. Of the Arizona desert she movingly captures the affirmative image of the "Little Okote Pine" (*Ocotillo*). The description of the desert, very succinct, communicates to the reader the impression of absolute emptiness, of a total negation. This is caught in an impressive lineal outline, purposely colorless.

> *Rasa patria, raso polvo,*
> *raso plexo del desierto . . .*

(See *Ocotillo* . . . on
p. 76 of this book)

Here too the tone is religious. The American cactus seems to her to be the only will that fights and opposes the destructive rule of Nothingness, manifesting instead emphatically, the creative *fiat* of God.

Ocotillo de Arizona	Little Okote of Arizona
sustentado en el desierto	Nourished in the desert
huesecillos requemados	Burnt little bones
crepitando y resistiendo,	Crackling and enduring,
tantos gestos aventados	So many gestures to the wind
y uno, y solo, y terco	And one, and alone, and
anhelo.	stubborn will.

With maternal tenderness she wishes to protect the small, defenseless plant mangled by the storm. She dries it, she straightens it, she runs her hand over it, as she dried, straightened, and ran her hand over the dead body of her Juan Miguel on that terrible night of his suicide.

The third poem, "Birth of a House" (*Nacimiento de una*

casa), describes the construction of a house near the sands of California. All the complicated work, the thousand diverse tasks are transformed into a marvelous game, into a truly joyful and profound creation. The birth of a house is like a spontaneous act of nature, in which light, air, the mysterious forces of the earth, and the guardian angels all take part. All the parts of the structure: posts, beams, doors, and windows are like the palpitating limbs of a living body in whose womb life will blossom with its joys and pains and "with a great death, standing on the threshold."

Here as well as in "California Poppy" (*Amapola de California*) and "Little Okote Pine" (*Ocotillo*), the material and mechanical work of building a house is filled with religious meaning. The house is not an instrument, nor a means. What is important is its end: the human life and destiny that will be fulfilled within it, beneath the gaze of God.

> Y *baja en un sesgo el Ángel*
> *Custodio de las moradas*
> *volca la mano diestra,*
> *jurándole su alianza*
> *y se la entrega a la costa*
> *en alta virgen dorada.*
>
> *En torno al bendecidor*
> *hierven cien cosas trocadas!*
> *fiestas, bodas, nacimientos,*
> *risas, bienaventuranzas,*
> *y se echa una Muerte grande,*
> *al umbral, atravesada . . .*
>   lines 37–48.

And calmly the Angel descends
Guardian of the houses
With a sweep of his right hand
Swearing his alliance
And he offers it to the shore
High as a golden virgin.

All about the blesser
Seethe a hundred transformed things;
Feasts, weddings, births,
Laughter, wishes for well-being,
And drawn up tall, a looming Death
Crossing on the threshold . . .

BIBLIOGRAPHY

A. *Poetry*
Antología. Selección de la propia autora. Pról. de Ismael Edwards
Mathe. Santiago de Chile, Zig-Zag, 1946.
Poesías completas. Recopilación de Margaret Bates. Estudio crítico-
bibliográfico de J. Saavedra Molina y un recuerdo lírico por Dulce
María Loynaz. Madrid, Aguilar, 1958.
Desolación. New York, Instituto de las Españas, 1922. 1era. edición.
Ternura. Madrid, Saturnino, Calleja, 1924, 1era. edición.
Nubes Blancas (poesías) y la *Oración de la Maestra.* Barcelona, B.
Bauzá, 1926? (Colección Apolo).
Tala. Buenos Aires, Sur, 1938. 1era. edición.
Lagar. Santiago de Chile, Editorial de Pacífico, 1954. 1era. edición.

B. *Prose*
Lecturas para mujeres. México, 1924.

C. *Articles by Gabriela Mistral on the United States*
El grito, Social, Santiago de Chile, mayo de 1922.
México y los Estados Unidos, Repertorio Americano, Costa Rica,
18 de septiembre de 1922.
Sobre panamericanismo, El Mercurio, Santiago de Chile, 10 de
junio de 1923.
Gabriela Mistral tiene la palabra, Boletín de la Unión Panamericana,
Washington, D. C., agosto de 1924.
El catolicismo en los Estados Unidos, El Mercurio, Santiago de
Chile, 27 de junio de 1924.
Cristianismo con sentido social, La Nueva Democracia, Nueva York,
julio de 1924.
Si Estados Unidos . . . , La Nueva Democracia, Nueva York, julio
de 1925.

149

Catolicismo y protestantismo, La Nueva Democracia, Nueva York, noviembre de 1925.

Estados Unidos y nosotros, La Nueva Democracia, Nueva York, marzo de 1927.

Contestación a una encuesta sobre una Sociedad de las Naciones americana, La Nueva Democracia, Nueva York, julio de 1927.

Balance de la hazaña americana: Una reivindicación yanqui, El Mercurio, Santiago de Chile, 7 de julio de 1927.

Sandino, Repertorio Americano, Costa Rica, 14 de abril de 1928.

La pobre ceiba, Repertorio Americano, Costa Rica, 19 de mayo de 1928.

Si Napoleón no hubiese existido, Repertorio Americano, Costa Rica, 19 de julio de 1928.

Información de la América Española en Estados Unidos, Puerto Rico Ilustrado, 22 de noviembre de 1930.

Antologías Indo-españolas en Estados Unidos, Puerto Rico Ilustrado, 27 de diciembre de 1930.

Cómo edifican, La Nueva Democracia, Nueva York, 7 de febrero de 1931.

Una amiga de los poetas sudamericanos: Alice Stone Blackwell, Puerto Rico Ilustrado, 14 de febrero de 1931.

La Estatua de la Liberted, Puerto Rico Ilustrado, 28 de febrero de 1931.

Voto a la juventud escolar en el Día de las Américas, Repertorio Americano, Costa Rica, 4 de abril de 1931.

Charles August Lindbergh, Puerto Rico Ilustrado, 6 de junio de 1931.

En defensa de la honra italiana, Puerto Rico Ilustrado, 13 de junio de 1931.

Elogio del pueblo italiano, Puerto Rico Ilustrado, 20 de junio de 1931.

La cacería de Sandino, Repertorio Americano, Costa Rica, 13 de julio de 1931.

Waldo Frank y nosotros, Repertorio Americano, Costa Rica, 5 de noviembre de 1932.

Mensaje a los estudiantes de español, Revista Hispánica Moderna, Nueva York, enero de 1937.

Unidad cristiana, La Nueva Democracia, Nueva York, marzo de 1944.

La buena fe, La Nueva Democracia, Nueva York, junio de 1944.

Coincidencias y disidencias entre las Américas, Revista América, Bogotá, febrero de 1945.

Palabras al Consejo Directivo de la Unión Panamericana, Boletín de la Unión Panamericana, Washington, D. C., junio de 1946.

La aventura de la lengua, Repertorio Americano, Costa Rica, 30 de junio de 1949.

Recuerdo del Dr. Rowe, Boletín de la Unión Panamericana, Washington, D. C., abril de 1947.

Sobre las cuidades númenes, El Mercurio, Santiago de Chile, 11 de marzo de 1948.

D. *Criticism on Gabriela Mistral*
Alone, *Gabriela Mistral*, Santiago de Chile, Nascimento, 1946.
Arce de Vázquez, Margot, *Gabriela Mistral: persona y poesía*, San Juan de Puerto Rico, Asomante, 1958.
Guillén de Nicolau, Palma, *El periodismo de Gabriela Mistral*, Conferencia, México, enero de 1958, págs. 3–18.
Guillén de Nicolau, Palma, *La varia poesía de Gabriela Mistral*, El Nacional, México, 25 de diciembre de 1949, 1 y 8 de enero de 1950.
Mañach, Jorge, *Gabriela: alma y tierra*, Revista Hispánica Moderna, 1937, III, núm. 2, págs. 106–110.
Rosenbaum, Sidonia C., *Criollismo y casticismo en Gabriela Mistral*, Cuadernos Americanos, 1953, XIII, núm. 1, págs. 296–300.
Saavedra Molina, Julio, *Gabriela Mistral: vida y obra*, Revista Hispánica Moderna, 1937, III, núm. 2, págs. 110+; Anales de la Universidad de Chile, 1946, CIV, núm. 63–64, págs. 23–104.
Valery, Paul, *Gabriela Mistral*, trad. de Luis Oyarzún, Atenea, Chile, 1947, LXXXVIII, págs. 313–322.
Vitier, Cintio, *La voz de Gabriela Mistral*, Santa Clara, Cuba, Universidad Central de las Villas, 1957.
Gabriela Mistral. Vida y obra. Bibliografía. Antología. New York, Instituto de las Españas, 1936.
Arrigoitia, Luis de, *Pensamiento y forma en la prosa de Gabriela Mistral*. Tesis presentada a la Facultad de Filosofía y Letras de la Universidad Central de Madrid para el grado de Doctor en junio de 1963. (En prensa: Edit. Gredos, Madrid).

E. *North American Criticism*
Adams, Mildred, *The 1945 winner of the Nobel award, Gabriela Mistral*. The New York Times, 9 of Dec., 1945.
Adams, Mildred, *Gabriela Mistral*. The Nation, 29 of Dec., 1945.
Bates, Margaret J., *Gabriela Mistral*, The Americas, 1946, III, pp. 168–189.
Bates, Margaret, *A propos an article on Gabriela Mistral*, América, 1957, XIV, pp. 145–157.
John Berchmans, Sister, *Gabriela Mistral and the Franciscan concept of life*, Renaissance, Renascence (Milwaukee) Wis., 1952, V. 40, 46, 95.
Blackwell, Alice S., *A Spanish-American poet*.
Espinosa, Aurelio M., *Gabriela Mistral*, The Americas, 1957, VIII, pp. 3, 40.
Feder, E., *Gabriela Mistral as I know her*. Books Abroad, 1946, XX, pp. 153–4.
Florit, Eugenio, *Paisaje y poesía en Gabriela Mistral*. Misceláneas de estudios a Joaquín de Carvalho, 1961, núm. 7, pp. 712–718.

152 BIBLIOGRAPHY

Onis, Harriet de, *Gabriela Mistral*. Rev. América, 1946, VI, pp. 3–7.
Pier, E. A., *Gabriela Mistral a tentative evaluation*. Rev. América, 1946, V, pp. 101–116.
Rosenbaum, Sidonia C., *Criollismo y Casticismo en Gabriela Mistral*. Cuadernos Americanos, 1953, XII, pp. 296, 300.
Sedgwick, Ruth, *Gabriela Mistral's Elqui Valley*, Hispania, 1952, XXXV, pp. 310–314.
Torres Rioseco, Arturo, *Ultimos recuerdos de Gabriela Mistral*. Insula, 1962, XVIII, pp. 1–16.
Mistral, Gabriela, *Selected poems*. Trans. Langston Hughes, Bloomington, Indiana Univ. Press, 1959.